Organizational Management and the COVID-19 Crisis

The COVID-19 pandemic has re-shaped organizations on many levels: resource, process, structural and relational. Such a wide range of forced changes has resulted in a greater need to implement risk management principles and procedures to secure an organization's position in the market. This book presents selected and key aspects of managing contemporary organizations in the conditions of the COVID-19 pandemic, enriched with empirical analyses relating to various countries of the world.

This edited collection focuses on clarifying and solving basic management dilemmas, integrated issues of risk management and organization security in light of changes during the COVID-19 pandemic. It specifically explores the following common problem areas, across industries and sectors, using theoretical, empirical and practical perspectives: financial, economic and regulatory conditions for management processes in the conditions of the COVID-19 pandemic; management of information resources and security in the conditions of the development of the phenomenon of digital risk and e-commerce; shaping relationships with stakeholders, with particular emphasis on relationships with customers in the conditions of sales processes; shaping the processes of creating and diffusing knowledge, with particular emphasis on the activities of educational entities.

Organizational Management and the COVID-19 Crisis will be directly relevant for researchers and academics across a range of management disciplines, including strategic management, risk management, organizational studies, information and knowledge management and related fields.

Wioletta Sylwia Wereda, PhD, is Doctor of Economics in the sciences of management and Associate Professor in Faculty of Security, Logistics and Management, Military University of Technology in Warsaw, Poland. She is the author of a variety of studies and business. She has also written and co-written three monographs and over 100 scientific articles in the field of management, published both in Poland and abroad. The scientific interests of Wioletta focus on the issues of modern and smart organizations, efficient stakeholder relationship management, sales management methods and new approach to the designing of relational sales. She is also a member of

Scientific Boards of International Journals (inter alia Management Dynamics in the Knowledge Economy, Hyperion International Journal of Econophysics and New Economy), and she is the Scientific Reviewer in different entities (the USA, Italy, Romania, Lithuania) and in Scientific Boards of National Journals.

Jacek Woźniak, PhD, is Doctor of Social Sciences in the discipline of management and quality. He is employed at the Institute of Organization and Management of the Military University of Technology in Warsaw, where for ten years he has been conducting research and teaching, among others, in the field of risk management, safety and efficiency in organizations, innovation management or process-based approach to management. He is the author or co-author of several scientific monographs and textbooks in the field of safety and risk management in organizations, and project and innovation management, as well as several dozen scientific articles.

Justyna Stochaj holds a PhD in Social Sciences at the Faculty of Security, Logistics and Management at the Military University of Technology. She deals with the problems of preparing the population for the occurrence of threats, the behavior of the population in crisis situations, as well as civil protection and civil defense.

Routledge Advances in Management and Business Studies

120 Consumer Packaging Strategy
Localisation in Asian Markets
Huda Khan, Richard Lee and Polymeros Chrysochou

121 Distress Risk and Corporate Failure Modelling
The State of the Art
Stewart Jones

122 Collaborative Leadership and Innovation
Management, Strategy and Creativity
Elis Carlström

123 Crowdsourcing for Innovation in Higher Education
Regina Lenart-Gansiniec and Łukasz Sułkowski

124 The Corporation of the Future
Edited by Stuart Orr and Paul Hunter

125 Organizational Management and the COVID-19 Crisis
Security and Risk Management Dilemmas
Edited by Wioletta Sylwia Wereda, Jacek Woźniak and Justyna Stochaj

126 Digital Entrepreneurship and the Global Economy
Edited by J. Mark Munoz

127 Cross-cultural Knowledge Management
Cultural Influences in China and Brazil
Jacky Hong and Jorge Muniz Jr.

For more information about this series, please visit: www.routledge.com/Routledge-Advances-in-Management-and-Business-Studies/book-series/SE0305

Organizational Management and the COVID-19 Crisis

Security and Risk Management Dilemmas

Edited by
Wioletta Sylwia Wereda, Jacek Woźniak and Justyna Stochaj

Routledge
Taylor & Francis Group
LONDON AND NEW YORK

First published 2022
by Routledge
4 Park Square, Milton Park, Abingdon, Oxon OX14 4RN

and by Routledge
605 Third Avenue, New York, NY 10158

Routledge is an imprint of the Taylor & Francis Group, an informa business

British Library Cataloguing-in-Publication Data
A catalogue record for this book is available from the British Library

ISBN: 978-1-032-25584-2 (hbk)
ISBN: 978-1-032-25933-8 (pbk)
ISBN: 978-1-003-28571-7 (ebk)

DOI: 10.4324/9781003285717

Typeset in Times New Roman
by codeMantra

Contents

List of charts ix
List of figures xi
List of tables xiii
Foreword xv
Editors xix

1 **Instruments supporting the economy of the European Union during the COVID-19 pandemic** 1
KONRAD STAŃCZYK

2 **Stability of public finance in Poland and the EU before and during the COVID-19 pandemic** 19
JANUSZ KOSTECKI

3 **Disinformation of the digital era revolution in conditions of COVID-19** 33
WIESŁAWA ZAŁOGA AND ROBERT MACIEJCZYK

4 **E-commerce market during the economic crisis caused by COVID-19** 44
MAŁGORZATA GRZELAK AND PAULINA OWCZAREK

5 **Customer evolution in terms of digital development and purchasing decisions during a pandemic security and risk** 65
WIOLETTA WEREDA, JACEK WOŹNIAK AND WOJCIECH WŁODARKIEWICZ

6 **Using the potential of the ISO 9001:2015 and ISO 22301:2019 standards in the fight against COVID-19** 86
MAŁGORZATA DĄBROWSKA-ŚWIDER

7 Acceptability and challenges of online higher education in the era of COVID-19 99
CELINA SOŁEK-BOROWSKA AND ADAM OSTANEK

8 Mitigating the risk of disruptions caused by the SARS-COV-2 pandemic by schools 110
KRZYSZTOF SZWARC AND MICHAŁ WIŚNIEWSKI

Index 127

Charts

3.1 Percentage distribution of responses to the question: based on the respondents' experiences over the past 6 months, which of the following forms of disinformation or manipulation did they most often experience? 38
3.2 Percentage distribution of answers to the question: how often do respondents come across information on the Internet that they believe was falsified or manipulated? 39
3.3 Percentage distribution of answers to the question: which of the following sources do respondents consider particularly conducive to spreading fake news? 41
3.4 Percentage distribution of answers to the question: using the Internet in the last three months, have checked credibility in terms of? 42
4.1 Search trends for the "online shopping" term in 2019 and 2020 48
4.2 Search popularity for the "online shopping" term in regions 49
4.3 Retail e-commerce sales worldwide by region, 2020 50
4.4 Box plot of the monthly mileage median depending on the vehicle brand 55
4.5 Box plot of the load weight median depending on the vehicle brand 55
4.6 Box plot of the revenue median depending on the vehicle brand 56
4.7 Average monthly mileage of vehicles in the company in individual months 56
4.8 Average monthly load weight of cargo transported by MAN vehicles in individual months 57
4.9 Average monthly weight of cargo transported by SCANIA vehicles in individual months 58
4.10 Average monthly weight of cargo transported by DAF vehicles in individual months 59
4.11 Average monthly revenue of the company in individual months 60
4.12 Answers to the question: do you actively use online shopping? 61
4.13 Answers to the question about the sales platforms and channels most often used by consumers 62

4.14 Categories of products most frequently purchased online 62
7.1 The structure of research sample – the criterion of university's faculty 103
7.2 Assessment of decision to incorporate online studying 104
7.3 Previous experience in online studying 105
7.4 Assessment of online studying 106
7.5 Platforms being used in online teaching 106
7.6 Barriers of students experience in online studying 107
7.7 The future of online studying 107
8.1 Children in the official school age range who are not enrolled in either primary or secondary school (in millions of people) 112
8.2 Cumulative number for 14 days of COVID-19 cases per 100,000 between 26.02. and 30.06.2020 116
8.3 Cumulative number for 14 days of COVID-19 cases per 100,000 between 01.07. and 30.11.2020 116

Figures

5.1 Internet evolution 69

5.2 New behaviours emerging across eight areas of consumer's life 76

Tables

2.1 Real GDP growth rate and inflation rate in the EU in 2018–2021 [in %] 21
2.2 General government revenues and expenditure in the EU in 2018–2019 [% of GDP] 25
2.3 Surplus/deficit and consolidated general government debt in the EU in 2008–2021 [% of GDP] 28
4.1 Value of the global e-commerce market in 2017–2023 49
4.2 Value of the e-commerce market in the USA in 2018–2022 50
4.3 Value of the e-commerce market in China in 2018–2024 50
4.4 Value of the e-commerce market in Germany in 2019–2023 51
4.5 Value of the e-commerce market in Canada in 2019–2024 51
4.6 Value of the e-commerce market in France in 2019–2023 51
4.7 Value of the e-commerce market in Latin America in 2018–2023 51
4.8 Variability of the average value of the daily mileage, load weight and revenue depending on the vehicle model 53
4.9 Results of the Kolmogorov–Smirnov test for the examined variables 54
4.10 The results of the Kruskal–Wallis test for individual variables 54
4.11 The results of the Kruskal–Wallis test for the significance of differences in the median load mass for individual months 57
4.12 The results of the Kruskal–Wallis test for the significance of differences in the median revenue for individual months 59
5.1 Factors influencing customer purchasing decisions during the pandemic 75
5.2 Client type (by age) 79
5.3 The level of the social technological ladder of the respondents (by age) 80
5.4 Digital risk perception 81
5.5 Factors building trust in client–entrepreneur relations 81
5.6 The level of consent to the indicated statements regarding the protection of personal data and privacy when making online purchases 82
7.1 Sample characteristics 103
8.1 Aggregate results of the assessment of the governmental support 117
8.2 SWOT analysis result 121

Foreword

The functioning conditions of contemporary organizations are particularly dynamic and unpredictable. It can be assumed that this statement is currently gaining importance and strength. In fact, in every sector of business and in every type of organization (commercial, public and social), changes are noticeable due to the continued development of the COVID-19 pandemic. Every aspect of these organizations' activities – including organizing resources, managing social capital, acquiring sources of financing for processes, shaping customer relations, sales – is currently conditioned by the limitations observed both on a global and local scale (i.e. in the economies of individual countries). In fact, the environment of most organizations (regardless of the region of the world) is no longer the same as it was before the pandemic, i.e. at the turn of 2020 and 2021. Moreover, it is assumed that these conditions will not change for a few (or even several) years. Organizations are forced to drastically change the way they think about their environment and to reevaluate their goals and interaction with external entities. The COVID-19 pandemic has (re) shaped the organization on many levels: resource, process, structural and relational. Such a wide range of changes in organizations (in fact forced changes) results in the need to implement risk management principles and procedures – which is an additional challenge for the organization and a source of additional threats that weaken the organization's potential to "fight" on the market. It is also worth noting that the (re)shaping of organizations in the conditions of the COVID-19 pandemic affects the level of security of these entities – in particular, economic security.

The primary purpose of this book is to identify the core areas of activity of organizations subject to (re)shaping under the COVID-19 pandemic. In addition, the book focuses on clarifying and solving basic management dilemmas, integrated issues of risk management and broadly understood organization security in various industries and sectors.

The book consists of eight chapters that explore the following problem areas:

- financial, economic and regulatory conditions for management processes in the conditions of the COVID-19 pandemic in various countries;

- management of information resources and security in the conditions of the development of the phenomenon of digital risk and e-commerce;
- shaping relationships with stakeholders – with particular emphasis on relationships with customers in the conditions of sales processes;
- shaping the processes of creating and diffusing knowledge, with particular emphasis on the activities of educational entities.

The aim of Chapter 1 is to characterize the instruments supporting the economy during the COVID-19 pandemic in selected countries. Germany, France and Italy were selected for the analysis as countries with highly developed economies in the EU, which are densely populated and severely affected by the consequences of the COVID-19 pandemic. Analyses, which are used in the elaboration, are as follows: selected literature from the scope of economical and society sciences, legislative acts of specifying instruments implementation for supporting the economy, general and governmental substantive elaborations concerning economic consequences of a pandemic, statistical data included in professional elaborations from the scope of proposed subject.

Chapter 2 presents the results of research on the medium-term financial situation of the general government sector in the European Union. The objective of the research is to determine the correlation between the economic situation, macroeconomic and health-related conditions, and the stability of public finances. The analysis covers the development of basic financial processes in the general government sector of individual EU member states, with particular emphasis on Poland, between 2018 and 2020, i.e. in the period before the pandemic and for the first months after its outbreak. Some basic trends and correlations are identified for the condition of the public finance sector during the economic boom (2018–2019) and after the outbreak of the pandemic. The author describes the impact of COVID-19 and the economic recession that the pandemic had brought about on such areas as revenues, expenses, financial result of the public finance sector and public debt. Also, on the basis of forecasts, possible directions of development of the financial situation for the years 2020–2021 are analyzed.

Chapter 3 shows that disinformation is the main reason for exerting a negative influence on human emotions, reasoning and behavior by creating a false image of reality. The development of new technologies has intensified the stubbornness with which disinformation can destabilize social environments. Manipulation of public opinion enhanced by new technologies has become possible on a very large scale. The phenomenon of disinformation, aimed at misleading public opinion, can be the cause of destabilization on many levels. Some are obvious, undermining state institutions, having destructive impact on its administrative and decision-making processes, as well as weakening the social, economic or cultural foundations. Since such activities are very common now, the purpose of this chapter is to discuss concerns related to the phenomenon of disinformation in the age of the digital revolution, with a particular focus on the security aspects. Principally, the awareness of the social environment in the area of knowledge concerning disinformation in the conditions of the COVID-19 pandemic is analyzed.

The aim of Chapter 4 is to analyze the potential opportunities and threats to the e-commerce industry related to the COVID-19 pandemic, to examine the dynamics of growth in the online sales volume of products as well as to determine the level of consumer satisfaction with online shopping and the possibility of switching to e-commerce from conventional sales channels.

Chapter 5 emphasizes that issues related to the digital age especially in recent years have become a very popular topic. Increased activity appearing around the creation of new technological solutions caused that humanity began to enter another era – the digital era. This phenomenon has started to affect not only consumers but also all business entities. Rapidly developing communication technologies and Internet applications have resulted in the need to adapt to emerging market trends. This chapter underlines that the digital age creates new, unprecedented opportunities for shopping, communication, exchange of large amounts of data, promotion, marketing and industry. Therefore, this chapter deals with a particularly important problem related to the development of shopping behavior, more focused on the digital system in the conditions of the COVID-19 pandemic.

Chapter 6 addresses the potential of the ISO 9001:2015 and ISO 22301:2019 standards in terms of increasing the level of security for various organizations and helping to minimize the threats posed by the COVID-19 pandemic. The main purpose of this chapter is to identify the parts of the above-mentioned standards that can be useful for this purpose and to give examples of possible applications that could allow modern organizations to respond to the challenges posed by the global pandemic. This chapter is purely theoretical in nature. In the research process, the author conducted an analysis of the available (mainly quantitative) statistical data, the data obtained from the survey and the ISO 9001:2015 and ISO 22301:2019 standards. Examination of the applicability of both standards in the fight against the threat of COVID-19 allowed to formulate the following hypothesis: taking advantage of the potential of the ISO 9001:2015 and ISO 22301:2019 standards may help to ensure security.

Chapter 7 examines how students in Poland had adjusted to the challenges of studying in online courses in the immediate aftermath of COVID-19 pandemic. The rise of online delivery of education has been well documented. However, experiences of students related to ad hoc movement to online classes due to pandemic outbreak have not been studied yet. What stands out in this experience is the role of online platforms in enabling online courses to be taught with faculty and students scattered over a wide geographical area. Both faculty and students had to learn very quickly how to instruct and take online courses. Many students felt that online courses offered flexibility and should remain an option to classroom instruction. This chapter indicates that students recommend blending learning and purely online teaching is not their preferred way of studying. Taking the benefits of online teaching, the university will have much better interactive courses using technology, building it into the classroom and adapting to a different economic landscape. For this experience, the university may actually come out as a better university in the future.

Chapter 8 aims to assess the business continuity strategies implemented in the education sector in selected EU member states. Pandemic like CoV-19 is a good example of Large Scale, Large Impact, Rare Event (LSLIRE). Identification, analysis and evaluation of such risk require custom approach. The uniqueness of such phenomena makes the common risk scales incomplete. With regard to these cases, risk has to be understood as a combination of the consequences of an event and the exposure to hazard. The CoV-19 pandemic shows that the scope of the risk mitigation strategy is strictly connected with many factors, including business sector specificity, especially if this activity is crucial for security and stability of the state. Susceptibility of risk mitigation strategy in each entity can be different, what should be taken into the consideration.

* * *

At this point, the Editors would like to thank all the authors of chapters and the entire community of the Faculty of Security, Logistics and Management of the Military University of Technology in Warsaw for their substantive support and constructive criticism of the monograph project at various stages of the research and analytical process.

Probably many issues from the presented area of considerations were not sufficiently illustrated in the book – but it results from certain methodological and formal limitations. Nevertheless, all not fully explored detailed problems will certainly be the subject of further research and publications by the authors of this volume.

We wish all readers a pleasant and useful reading!

– Editors: Wioletta Wereda, Jacek Woźniak and Justyna Stochaj

Editors

Justyna Stochaj, PhD, is Associate Professor in Faculty of Security, Logistics and Management at the Military University of Technology in Warsaw, Poland. She is the author of articles about civilian security. The scientific interests of Justyna Stochaj focus on the issues of civil protection and civil defense, security management as well as individual protection of the population and people's behavior in emergency situations.

Wioletta Wereda, PhD, is Doctor of Economics in the sciences of management and Associate Professor in Faculty of Security, Logistics and Management at the Military University of Technology in Warsaw, Poland. She is the author of a variety of studies and business. She has also written and co-written three monographs and over 100 scientific articles in the field of management, published both in Poland and abroad. The scientific interests of Wioletta focus on the issues of modern and smart organizations, efficient stakeholder relationship management, sales management methods and new approach to the designing of relational sales. She is also a member of Scientific Boards of International Journals (inter alia Management Dynamics in the Knowledge Economy, Hyperion International Journal of Econophysics and New Economy), and she is the Scientific Reviewer in different entities (the USA, Italy, Romania, Lithuania) and in Scientific Boards of National Journals.

Jacek Woźniak, PhD, is Doctor of Social Sciences in the discipline of management and quality. He is employed at the Institute of Organization and Management of the Military University of Technology in Warsaw, Poland, where for ten years he has been conducting research and teaching, among others, in the field of risk management, safety and efficiency in organizations, innovation management or process-based approach to management. He is the author or co-author of several scientific monographs and textbooks in the field of safety and risk management in organizations, and project and innovation management, as well as several dozen scientific articles.

1 Instruments supporting the economy of the European Union during the COVID-19 pandemic

Konrad Stańczyk

Introduction

The SARS-COV-2 virus causing the COVID-19 disease was first detected in December 2019 in the Chinese city of Wuhan. Due to the speed and ease of movement of the virus as well as its mode of transmission, the pandemic rapidly spread across the globe, and Europe became its epicentre.

The COVID-19 pandemic in 2020 is the first crisis of its kind. It affects all countries and impacts all areas of social, economic and cultural activities. For societies, nations, countries and individual citizens, this phenomenon is new, unknown and consequently dangerous and paralysing. The threat posed by a pandemic is primarily of medical importance, deciding on infection, diseases and, unfortunately, often human life. Nevertheless, a number of other threats and limitations are also significant, including those related to the economic activity. For many businesses, the COVID-19 pandemic is a period of real attempt to survive, where the previous rules of the market economy proved to be unreliable. In this difficult period for businesses, the states took over some restrictions and proposed specific solutions supporting the activities of individual economic entities as well as the national economy as a whole. This is particularly important for selected branches, such as communication, transport, health services, hospitality and cosmetics industries as well as those related to broadly understood culture or trade.

The aim of this study is to characterise the instruments supporting the economy during the COVID-19 pandemic in selected countries. Germany, France and Italy were selected for the analysis as countries with highly developed economies in the European Union (EU), which are densely populated and severely affected by the consequences of the COVID-19 pandemic (World Economic Outlook Database, 2020).

Analyses, which will be used in the elaboration, are as follows: selected literature from the scope of economical and society sciences, legislative acts of specifying instruments implementation for supporting the economy, general and governmental substantive elaborations concerning economic consequences of a pandemic, statistical data included in professional elaborations from the scope of proposed subject.

DOI: 10.4324/9781003285717-1

Measures taken by the European Union to protect the economy

As a result of the COVID-19 pandemic, which poses a serious threat to the public health and significantly affects citizens, societies and economies, the EU is faced by a historic socio-economic challenge. This is due to the fact that the COVID-19 pandemic is associated with a significant human aspect. It brings significant social consequences and at the same time causes a serious shock to the global and European economy.

This shock is affecting the economy through different channels (Coordinated Economic Response to the COVID-19 Outbreak, 2020):

1 The shock resulting from China's initial contraction in the first quarter of 2020;
2 The supply shock to the European and global economy resulting from the disruption of supply chains' absences from the workplace;
3 The demand shock to the European and global economy caused by lower consumer demand and the negative impact of uncertainty on investment plans;
4 The impact of liquidity constraints for firms.

The spread of the virus is causing disruption of global supply chains, volatility in financial markets, consumer demand shocks and negative impact in key sectors like travel and tourism.

Counterbalancing the socio-economic effects of the COVID-19 outbreak requires bold actions taken timely and in a coordinated way by all EU decision makers. To this end, Europe is working on all fronts to contain the spread of the coronavirus, support national health systems and counter the socio-economic impact of the pandemic with unprecedented measures at both national and EU level. In addition in order to facilitate immediate relief to hard-hit SMEs, the EU budget will deploy its existing instruments in order to support them with liquidity, complementing measures taken at the national level.

To reduce the socio-economic impact of the COVID-19 pandemic to a minimum as well as to restore sustainable economic development, the EU has implemented a package of measures, including:

1 Structural funds for the Member States from the cohesion fund under the cohesion policy programmes for 2014–2020 – EUR 37 billion;
2 Funds for the Member States from the European Union Solidarity Fund – EUR 800 million;
3 Funds for dealing with the crisis caused by COVID-19 – EUR 3.1 billion;
4 Funds from the European Investment Fund as part of the EU budget guarantee to ensure liquidity to enterprises – aid for at least 100,000 businesses – EUR 8 billion;

5 SURE instrument[1] to protect workplaces and workers through an array of preferential loans – EUR 100 billion. These funds are to be used for loans to countries, which require subsidies for programmes that will keep people in employment and limit mass layoffs (solutions enabling the reduction of working time or similar ones protecting against loss of income and employment, including those for self-employed). The SURE instrument is supposed to utilise the elements of financial engineering to reduce the cost of floatation (Grzeszak, Leśniewicz, Śliwowski, Święcicki, 2020);
6 Flexibility in the application of EU regulations concerning the expenditure of funds from the European funds, enabling free disposal of amounts allocated to each country (without limitations in terms of shifting between specific objectives, regions or funding sources). The obligation to co-finance from national funds has also been abolished. Under this provision, the Member States could use funds from:

   - The European Regional Development Fund and the European Social Fund for investments in healthcare systems
   - The European Social Fund to temporarily support national part-time working schemes
   - The European Maritime and Fisheries Fund to protect the income of fishermen and aquaculture farmers affected by the crisis

7 Flexibility of the fiscal rules to help national authorities in offering financial support to healthcare systems and businesses as well as in maintaining employment during the crisis;
8 The European Investment Bank guarantee funds for small and medium-sized businesses in a particularly difficult situation as financial liquidity support measures in emergency situations – EUR 200 billion;
9 Funds from the European Central Bank under the Pandemic Emergency Purchase Programme (PEPP) for the purchase of private and public securities during the crisis – EUR 750 billion;
10 The banking package to facilitate lending to households and businesses in the entire EU;
11 Postponing the entry of two EU tax measures into force, i.e. the VAT e-commerce package and the submission and exchange of information in accordance with the Directive on Administrative Cooperation (DAC);

Furthermore, on 27 May 2020, the European Commission proposed a recovery fund called the "Next Generation EU", in which subsidies and loans for each EU Member State amount to EUR 500 billion and EUR 250 billion, respectively. This followed extensive negotiations, in which the so-called "Frugal Five", including the Netherlands, Austria, Denmark, Sweden and Finland, rejected the idea of giving away cash in the form of grants, preferring loans instead. According to the proposal, the money raised on the capital market will be returned in the years 2028–2058, and thus will translate into the standard of living and debt of future generations (https://ec.europa.eu/info/live-work-travel-eu/health/coronavirus-response/recovery-plan-europe_pl, 2020).

However, it is worth noting that the main part of the main fiscal response to the coronavirus comes from Member States' national budgets. The European Commission adopted temporary state aid rules so governments can provide liquidity to the economy to support citizens and save jobs. Commission has adopted over 200 decisions approving national measures, such as guarantee schemes for companies and funds to support the production and supply of medical devices (Overview of the Commission's Response, an Official Website of the European Union, 2020).

Protective measures for national economies

Given the limited size of the EU budget, the main fiscal response to the coronavirus will come from Member States' national budgets. EU State aid rules enable Member States to take swift and effective action to support citizens and companies, in particular SMEs, facing economic difficulties due to the COVID-19 outbreak.

Member States have already adopted or are adopting budgetary, liquidity and policy measures to increase the capacity of their health systems and provide relief to those citizens and sectors that are particularly impacted.

Under EU State aid rules, i.e. the Commission's Rescue and Restructuring Guidelines based on Article 107(3)(c) TFEU, Member States are able to grant urgent and temporary assistance in the form of loan guarantees or loans to all types of companies in difficulty. Such aid would cover companies' expected operating needs for a six-month period. In addition, companies that are not (yet) in difficulty can also receive such support, if they face acute liquidity needs due to exceptional and unforeseen circumstances such as the COVID-19 outbreak, in compliance with relevant conditions, notably with regard to the level of remuneration that the beneficiary is required to pay for the State guarantee or loan. Furthermore, the Rescue and Restructuring Guidelines enable Member States to put in place dedicated support schemes for SMEs and smaller state-owned companies, including to cover their acute liquidity needs for a period of up to 18 months (COM, 2020).

Member States can design ample support measures in line with existing State aid rule. First, Member States can decide to take measures applicable to all companies, for example wage subsidies and suspension of payments of corporate and value-added taxes or social contributions. These measures alleviate financial strains on companies in a direct and efficient manner. They fall outside the scope of State aid control and can be put in place by Member States immediately, without involvement of the

Commission. Second, Member States can grant financial support directly to consumers, e.g. for cancelled services or tickets that are not reimbursed by the operators concerned. These measures also fall outside the scope of State aid control and can be put in place by Member States immediately, without involvement of the Commission. Third, State aid rules based on Article 107(3)(c) TFEU enable Member States, subject to Commission approval, to meet acute liquidity needs and support companies facing bankruptcy due to the COVID-19 outbreak. Fourth, Article 107(2)(b) TFEU enables Member States, subject to Commission approval, to compensate companies for the damage suffered in exceptional circumstances, such as those caused by the COVID-19 outbreak. This includes measures to compensate companies in sectors that have been particularly hard hit (e.g. transport, tourism and hospitality) and measures to compensate organisers of cancelled events for damages suffered due to the outbreak (Annexes to the Communication from the Commission to the European Parliament, 2020).

Germany

In response to the COVID-19 pandemic, the federal cabinet adopted a supplementary budget for 2020 on 23 March 2020. After it was passed by the Bundestag on 25 March 2020, the supplementary budget entered into force with retroactive effect as of 1 January 2020. The supplementary budget provides for net borrowing of €156.0 billion. The supplementary budget is based on the government's updated expectations for the economy's performance (compared with the January annual projection) and draws on the experiences gained during the financial and economic crisis of 2009. The expected declines in Federation, Länder and local authority tax revenue were determined on this basis. In addition to the supplementary budget, the Bundestag also passed the Economic Stabilisation Fund Act (Gesetz zur Errichtung eines Wirtschaftsstabilisierungsfonds, 2020). Furthermore, additional legislation has been adopted in response to the COVID-19 pandemic in order to expand social security and strengthen the healthcare system (German Stability Programme, 2020).

To protect their own economy, the German authorities introduced a number of systemic solutions based on three basic concepts, i.e. the direct fiscal impulse, deferrals as well as other liquidity and guarantee measures.

The direct fiscal impulse includes (Śmigiel, Łyjak, 2020):

1 Recapitalisation and purchase of shares in companies affected by the virus via the Economic Stabilisation Fund – EUR 100 billion;
2 Pandemic control projects, including a hospital fund for covering any income-incurred losses or higher costs – EUR 55 billion;
3 Direct grants for supporting sole proprietorships and microenterprises – EUR 50 billion;

4 Maintaining employment positions by extending the reduced employee benefits programme – EUR 10 billion;
5 Extending access to social benefits (per child, for people with disabilities), abolishing the rules for determining income criterion and inclusion of people who are self-employed – EUR 7.7 billion;
6 Additional expenses for statutory health insurance and long-term health insurance – EUR 5.2 billion;
7 Emergency measures, such as the purchase of protective suits and face coverings, research into vaccines against SARS-COV-2 and ensuring the return of German holidaymakers left abroad – EUR 3.7 billion;
8 Additional investment in the private sector – EUR 3.1 billion per year in the years 2021–2024;
9 Extending venture capital financing of start-ups, tech businesses and small companies affected by the coronavirus crisis – EUR 2 billion.

During the current pandemic, the German government has reached for a solution that has been present in the German law for almost 100 years, extending its scope and scale. The term "Kurzarbeitergeld", which refers to the salary of an employee temporarily working shorter hours, appeared in the regulations in 1924. It means that the state provides support in the payment of wages to employees when a company lacks orders. Under these circumstances, employees work shorter hours and the company is compensated for the parts of the wages exceeding the new working hours (60% of the difference between the basic working time and the reduced working time) (Grzeszak, Leśniewicz, Śliwowski, Święcicki, 2020) after proving a decrease in revenue to the Federal Employment Agency. These enhancements entered into force on 1 March 2020 with a retroactive effect and have an estimated effect of EUR 10.1 billion on the budget of the Federal Labour Office (Policy Measures Taken against the Spread and Impact of the Coronavirus, 2020).

The changes effective from March of this year include (Die Bundesregierung, 2020):

1 Entitling the company to claim compensation when the percentage of workers at risk of dismissal equals 10% (down from 30%),
2 Suspension of social security payments for employees eligible for Kurzarbeitergeld,
3 Covering temporary workers with the scheme as well,
4 Accelerating the possibility of participating in the scheme without the need for a negative working time balance (i.e. a period of no orders).

Deferrals essentially cover two main directions, specifically the deferral of direct corporate income tax – EUR 70 billion, and the deferral of indirect taxes and social security contributions – EUR 430 billion.

Other liquidity and guarantee measures adopted in Germany include (Policy Measures Taken against the Spread and Impact of the Coronavirus, 2020):

1 Extending the existing federal guarantees and creating new ones – EUR 366.5 billion;
2 Ensuring guarantees and solving liquidity problems under the Economic Stabilization Fund (ESM) – EUR 400 billion;
3 Refinancing of large loans – EUR 100 billion;
4 Measures implemented at the federal state level:

   - Extension of the guarantee framework – EUR 63.2 billion;
   - Loans – EUR 12.7 billion.

France

The French economy, which is the EU's second largest economy, experienced a decrease by 13.8% in the second quarter of 2020 compared to the first three months of the year and by 19% compared to the same quarter of the previous year. This is the country's worst recession since the Second World War. According to forecasts, the annual decrease is expected to reach approximately 11%.

In response to the crisis, the authorities prepared a generous public aid plan. Additionally, they also want to take advantage of the situation to reduce the industry's dependence on foreign partners.

The French government has already allocated EUR 450 billion to save the economy during the crisis caused by the coronavirus epidemic. This is the equivalent of 20% of the country's gross domestic product (GDP).

In response to the COVID-19 pandemic and as part of a coordinated EU approach, France has adopted timely budgetary measures to increase the capacity of its health system, halt the pandemic as well as to help particularly affected individuals and sectors. The 2020 stability programme indicates that these budgetary measures represent 1.9% of the GDP. They include financing of the reduced-time employment programme (1.1% of the GDP), additional expenditure to strengthen the health services, covering relief from health insurance contributions and medical staff salaries (0.4% of the GDP) and the creation of a solidarity fund to provide direct support to small and very small businesses as well as to people who are self-employed (0.3% of the GDP).

France launched the first aid packages as early as in mid-March. They comprised state-subsidised time off, business loans, tax deferrals or company relief measures, among others. The aid included (Śmigiel, Łyjak, 2020):

1 Funds for the national health system for the necessary materials and compensation for health workers – EUR 8 billion;

2. Financial support for employees for two months (partial coverage of their remuneration) – EUR 24 billion;
3. Funds for hospitals from unspent reserves of the 2019 budget – EUR 3.76 billion;
4. Grants through the Solidarity Fund to small businesses with a revenue of less than EUR 1 million, which lost 50% or more of their revenue in March 2020, as well as to the self-employed and micro entrepreneurs – EUR 7 billion;
5. Plan supporting start-ups – EUR 2 billion.

Despite a double-digit recession in the second quarter, thanks to the rapid implementation of the rescue plan, the French economy has managed to avoid a wave of bankruptcies and mass unemployment as a result of the spring quarantine. On the 3rd of September 2020, the French government presented the assumptions of a new aid plan called "France Relance", worth as much as EUR 100 billion, 40 billion of which will come from the funds received by France under the EU Reconstruction Fund. The financing of "France Relance" is to be made possible by the rapid restoration of the economic growth and is to be implemented without any increase in taxes.

The package is to be divided into three pillars. The first pillar, which amounts to EUR 35 billion, will be linked to improving the competitiveness of companies and the economy as a whole. Of this sum, EUR 20 billion will be used for tax relief for the manufacturing sector over the next two years as well as for contribution relief. The government will spend EUR 11 billion on investments, reindustrialisation and digitisation of businesses, while EUR 3 billion will go to businesses particularly affected by the economic impact of the epidemic. Even before the pandemic, liquidity problems related to payment bottlenecks were a chronic problem for small and medium-sized French businesses (SMBs). The French government believes that there is too much fragmentation of subcontractors in sectors that are crucial for the French economy (e.g. armaments, aviation and space industries) and that consolidation is needed. It is intended to prepare the economy for the consolidation policy, which France also advocates at the European level. That is why the main tools to support SMBs as part of the recovery plan are thought to be exchangeable bonds and participating loans to facilitate the buyout of businesses. The latter, financed by the state investment bank Bpifrance, should not only support SMB investments (from the EUR 3 billion allocated for this purpose, the state wants to obtain up to EUR 15 billion of added value), but should also enable the state to block the acquisition of strategically important start-ups by foreign entities (Maślanka, 2020).

The French authorities believe that the current decade will shape the production and development trends for the subsequent decades. This is connected to the energy transition and other measures aimed at achieving climate neutrality by 2050. Appropriate preparation for these challenges, while maintaining the competitiveness of the economy, requires investments, for which EUR 30 billion has been allocated to the "France Relance" programme (Maślanka, 2020). These funds will be used for purposes related to the energy transition, including support for transport (EUR 11 billion), transformation of businesses (EUR 9 billion), soil fertilisation (EUR 1.3 billion) as well as renovation of buildings (EUR 6.7 billion) and investments related to hydrogen energy (EUR 7 billion).

The third pillar is the maintenance of social cohesion. EUR 35 billion will be allocated for this purpose. The government's priority will be to save jobs and as much as EUR 15 billion will be allocated for this purpose. EUR 6.7 billion will be invested in youth employment support programmes, while EUR 7.6 billion will go to companies to prevent redundancies (Krzysztoszek, Stam, 2020). Intriguingly, the two-year French plan focuses on strengthening companies rather than on the direct support to increase the customer demand. It is assumed that next year, the scheme will contribute to the creation of 160,000 new workplaces and the economic growth in France is expected to regain its 2019 level in 2022.

Italy

In the second half of March 2020, Italy became a country with the highest death toll caused by COVID-19 in the world. The main reason for this was the high proportion of people in the Italian society considered to be at risk of increased COVID-19 morbidity. People over 60 years old constitute 29% of the Italian population and the average age in Italy is equal to 44.7 years old. This makes Italy the second eldest society in the world (after Japan). Concurrently, speculation about new restrictions to be introduced caused people (frequently unaware carriers of the coronavirus) to panic and relocate from the northern to the southern parts of the country. Moreover, the postponement of decisions regarding movement restrictions and conducting economic activities caused people to transmit the virus during visits in clubs or restaurants. As of the 25th of March, nearly 70,000 people were infected and 6,800 people died due to COVID-19 (Pawłowski, 2020).

Since March, three fiscal packages, amounting to EUR 100.3 billion (equivalent to 6.3% of the GDP), have been introduced by the Italian government. They affect the 2020 budget and they are aimed at reducing the negative impacts of the pandemic (Policy Measures Taken against the Spread and Impact of the Coronavirus, 2020).

1 Law Decree no. 18 from 17 March ('Cura Italia' decree) containing measures to strengthen the national health system and for the economic support of households, workers and firms – EUR 20 billion,
2 Law Decree no. 34 from 19 May ('Recovery' decree) containing measures on healthcare, economy, jobs and social policies – EUR 55.3 billion,

3 Law Decree no. 104 from 14 August ('August' decree) adopting a more selective approach in measures, including some forward-looking elements – EUR 25 billion.

As a result of the pandemic, already in the beginning of the crisis in Italy, in March 2020, the authorities took steps aimed at saving the economy and workplaces. To this end, the following solutions were implemented (Śmigiel, Łyjak, 2020):

1 All companies in sectors severely affected by COVID-19 (tourism and entertainment, transportation, hospitality, culture, sport, education, public events) as well as companies under EUR 2 million were granted reductions in taxes and compulsory contributions (in total EUR 2.4 billion);
2 Terminations of employment contracts, regardless of their type, were frozen for two months if they were handed after 23rd February. This included economic redundancies;
3 Unemployment insurance systems were expanded for all sectors, regions and employees;
4 Self-employed people conducting economic activity were to receive a grant of EUR 600;
5 All employees, who do not work remotely, were to be granted a EUR 100 salary bonus (upper income limit – EUR 40,000);
6 A EUR 600 bonus was established for employed parents.

As of October 2020, in Italy, the employment support, including that for people who are self-employed, amounts to EUR 27 billion and comprises the following (Conte, Gualtieri, 2020; Policy Measures Taken against the Spread and Impact of the Coronavirus, 2020):

1 Approximately EUR 19 billion as wage supplementation schemes aimed to safeguard jobs in all their variations (ordinary, extraordinary and in derogation), which are available to all businesses. Through the subsequent decrees, these schemes were extended until the end of 2020.
2 Approximately EUR 8 billion was allocated to the support of the self-employed and freelancers through various schemes:

   - an allowance of EUR 600 for the months of March and April 2020 for self-employed persons and freelancers;
   - an allowance of EUR 600 for the month of March 2020 and of EUR 500 for the month of April 2020 for fixed-term employees in agriculture; an allowance of EUR 600 for the months of March, April and May 2020 for workers in the entertainment industry (with annual income up to EUR 50,000); an allowance of EUR 600 for the months of March, April and May 2020 for collaborators of sports associations; an allowance of EUR 600 for the months of March, April and

May 2020 for on-call workers and an allowance of EUR 500 for the months of April and May 2020 for domestic workers.
- non-repayable grants for self-employed workers and individual enterprises.

3 The August decree introduced a new 1,000 € one-off allowance for some of the workers who benefited by the former allowance (seasonal workers in the tourism, entertainment and other sectors, other atypical employees) and the lower allowances for the sport and the shipping sector were extended.

Other expenditure:

1 Around EUR 7.5 billion in other forms of income support, including various social benefits such as:

- paid leave for persons affected by disabilities or for caregivers who assist people affected by disabilities until June; sick leave for people in quarantine until July;
- parental leave benefits for up to 30 days in the period from 5 March 2020 to 31 August 2020;
- baby-sitting vouchers for a maximum of EUR 2,000 as an alternative to parental leave benefits and valid for the same period;
- extra unemployment benefits for those who see their ordinary income support expire in May and June;

2 Around EUR 12 billion in transfers to regional and local governments to compensate for the decline in revenues from own and shared taxes;
3 Around EUR 1.5 billion for the education system, including the reopening of schools;
4 Around EUR 11 billion in support for the loss compensation of firms;
5 Around EUR 7.5 billion in support to various sectors (tourism, culture, transport, innovation, climate, etc.);
6 Around EUR 8 billion as public guarantee provisions;
7 EUR 20 billion for abrogation of the VAT safeguard clauses in 2021.
8 EUR 4 billion for the abrogation of the regional tax on productive activities (IRAP) due in 2020;
9 EUR 0.5 billion as exemptions from social security contributions, for up to four months until the end of 2020;
10 EUR 1.5 billion as temporary reduction of 30% of the social security contributions paid by employers on employment contracts based in a region of the South in October–December 2020.
11 Around EUR 2 billion in other tax cuts, including:

- Exemption from first and second instalment of the property tax (IMU) for 2020 for reception and entertainment facilities. Extension of the exemption to 2021 and 2022 for cinemas and theatres.

- Exemption from ground occupation taxes (TOSAP and COSAP) until 31 December 2020.
- Extension to 2021 of existing tax breaks for firms that undertake a new economic initiative in the areas of central Italy affected by the 2016 earthquake;
- Tax credit of 60% of the rent for the months of March, April and May for businesses and self-employed up to 5 million revenues who recorded a 50% drop in March, April and May turnover. Hotels, agritourist facilities and other touristic facilities can take advantage of the credit regardless of the size and turnover reduction;
- Tax credit for holidays (for households with yearly income below EUR 40,000).
- Exemption from VAT on protection and safety devices in 2020, and reduction to 5% VAT afterwards.

12 Around EUR 6 billion in various tax deferrals.

Recovery plan for Europe

To help repair the economic and social damage brought by the coronavirus pandemic, kick-start European recovery and protect and create jobs, the European Commission proposed on 26 May a major recovery plan for Europe based on harnessing the full potential of the EU budget. On 21 July 2020, the EU leaders agreed on this recovery plan and the multiannual financial framework for 2021–2027, leading the way out of the crisis and laying foundations for a modern and more sustainable Europe. Negotiations with the European Parliament will now follow with a view to urgently finalising the work on all legal acts (Recovery Plan for Europe, an Official Website of the European Union, 2020). EU leaders have agreed to a package of €1.8 trillion which combines the next budget and Next Generation EU. Under the agreement, the Commission will be able to borrow up to €750 billion on the markets (Overview of the Commission's Response, an Official Website of the European Union, 2020).

To mobilise the necessary investments, the Commission is putting forward a two-fold response:

1 Next Generation EU is a new recovery instrument of €750 billion which will boost the EU budget with new financing raised on the financial markets for 2021–2024.
2 A reinforced long-term budget of the EU for 2021–2027 (€1,100 billion).

Next Generation EU of €750 billion as well as targeted reinforcements to the long-term EU budget for 2021–2027 will bring the total financial firepower of the EU budget to €1.85 trillion. Together with the three important safety nets for workers, businesses and sovereigns endorsed by the European Council on 23 April 2020 and amounting to a package worth €540 billion, these exceptional measures taken at the EU level would reach more than €1.290 trillion (The EU Budget Powering the Recovery Plan for Europe, 2020). Every programme and every euro mobilised under Next Generation EU will be used to tackle the most crucial recovery needs of the EU Member States and their partners. The funds will go to where they can make the greatest difference, complementing and amplifying the essential work under way in the Member States (Key Instruments Supporting the Recovery Plan for Europe, 2020).

The investments under Next Generation UE will be channelled via a variety of instruments under three pillars (Key Instruments Supporting the Recovery Plan for Europe, 2020):

1 Supporting Member States to recover, repair and emerge stronger from the crisis,

  1.1 Recovery and Resilience facility,
   - To be used for: Investments and reforms, including in green and digital transitions;
   - Mechanism: Grants and loans by implementing Member States' national recovery and resilience plans defined in line with the objectives of the European Semester, including in relation to the green and digital transitions and the resilience of national economies;
   - Budget: €560 billion of which €310 billion for grants and €250 billion in loans;
   - Distribution key: Available to all Member States, focus on the most affected countries;

  1.2 Recovery Assistance for Cohesion and the Territories of Europe – REACT-EU (Additional funding in 2020–2022 for the current cohesion programmes as well as for the Fund for European Aid to the Most Deprived);
   - To be used for: Employment subsidies, short time work schemes and youth employment measures; liquidity and solvency for SMEs.
   - Mechanism: Flexible cohesion policy grants for municipalities, hospitals, companies via Member States' managing authorities. No national co-financing required;
   - Budget: €55 billion of additional cohesion policy funding between 2020 and 2022;
   - Distribution key: Focus on the most affected countries and regions, taking into account the severity of the economic and social impacts of the crisis, including the level of youth unemployment and the relative prosperity of Member States;

1.3 Reinforced rural development programmes,
- A €15 billion reinforcement for the European Agricultural Fund for Rural Development to support rural areas in making the structural changes necessary in line with the European Green Deal and achieving the ambitious targets in line with the new Biodiversity and Farm to Fork strategies;

1.4 Reinforced Just Transition Mechanism,
- A proposal to strengthen the Just Transition Fund up to €40 billion, to assist Member States in accelerating the transition towards climate neutrality

2 Kick-starting the economy and helping private investment to get moving again,

2.1 Solvency Support Instrument (new instrument to support equity of viable companies which suffer due to the coronavirus crisis);
- To be used for: Equity support to viable companies from all economic sectors to address solvency concerns, caused by the coronavirus pandemic, and help them through their green and digital transformation;
- Mechanism: Provisioning of an EU budget guarantee to the European Investment Bank Group in order to mobilise private capital (via financial intermediaries, for example independently managed funds or Special Purpose Vehicles);
- Budget: €31 billion;
- Distribution key: Demand driven and available to all Member States, focus on those particularly hit by the coronavirus crisis, which are less able to intervene through national state aid, in the most affected sectors;

2.2 Enhanced Invest EU (including a Strategic Investment Facility);
- To be used for: Investments in sustainable infrastructure, R&I and digitisation, SMEs and midcaps, social investment and skills across the EU. In addition, the new Strategic Investment Facility will aim to develop strong and resilient independent value chains such as critical infrastructure, green and digital technologies and healthcare and enhance the autonomy of the Union's single market;
- Mechanism: Provisioning of an EU budget guarantee for financing of investment projects via the EIB group and national promotional banks;
- Budget: €15.3 billion for InvestEU. Additionally, a new Strategic Investment Facility to be equipped with €15 billion provisioning from Next Generation EU;
- Distribution key: Demand driven and available to all Member States;

3 Learning the lessons of the crisis and addressing Europe's strategic challenges.

   3.1 New Health programme (new programme, respecting the division of competences between the Union and Member States in this field, to help equip Europe against future health threats);
   - To be used for: Investments in EU healthcare systems with a focus on:
     - health security and capacity to react to crises;
     - long-term disease prevention and surveillance, health access, diagnosis and treatment, cross-border collaboration in the health domain;
   - Mechanism: Grants directly to beneficiaries by the European Commission, centrally managed procurements by the European Commission;
   - Budget: €9.4 billion;
   - Distribution key: Centrally managed programme benefiting all Member States;

   3.2 Reinforced rescue (reinforcement of the Union's civil protection support capacity to respond to large-scale emergencies);
   - To be used for: Health emergencies response infrastructure: storage capacity, systems to transport medicines, doctors and patients within the EU or to bring them in from outside the EU;
   - Mechanism: Grants and procurements managed by the European Commission;
   - Budget: A total of €3.1 billion;
   - Distribution key: Centrally managed programme benefiting all Member States.

The Commission is also proposing to reinforce other programmes to allow them to play their full role in making the Union more resilient and addressing challenges brought along by the pandemic and its consequences (Key Instruments Supporting the Recovery Plan for Europe, 2020):

1 A total of €94.4 billion for Horizon Europe, to increase European support for health and climate-related research and innovation activities;
2 A total of €87 billion for the Neighbourhood, Development and International Cooperation Instrument, via a new External Action Guarantee and the European Fund for Sustainable Development to support partners – in particular in the Western Balkans, the Neighbourhood and the rest of Africa – in their efforts to fight and recover from the impact of the pandemic;
3 An increase of €5 billion for the Humanitarian Aid Instrument, reflecting growing humanitarian needs in the most vulnerable parts of the world;

4. A total of €8.2 billion for Digital Europe programme to boost the Union's cyberdefences and support the digital transition;
5. Investing in an up-to-date, high-performance transport infrastructure to facilitate cross-border connections, such as Rail Baltica, through an additional €1.5 billion for the Connecting Europe Facility;
6. Creating the conditions for a well-functioning single market driving recovery by maintaining the proposed budgets for the Single Market Programme and for programmes supporting cooperation in the fields of taxation and customs at a level of €3.7 billion, €239 million and €843 million, respectively;
7. A top-up of €3.4 billion for Erasmus Plus bringing the total to €24.6 billion to invest in young people, as well as in the cultural and creative sectors through an increase of Creative Europe to a level of €1.5 billion;
8. An increase of €4 billion for the Common Agricultural Policy and of €500 million for the European Maritime and Fisheries Fund, to strengthen the resilience of the agri-food and fisheries sectors and to provide the necessary scope for crisis management;
9. A total of €22 billion for the Asylum and Migration Fund and Integrated Border Management Fund, to step up cooperation on external border management as well as migration and asylum policy;
10. A total of €2.2 billion for the Internal Security Fund and a total of €8 billion for the European Defence Fund to support the European strategic autonomy and security;
11. A total of €12.9 billion for pre-accession assistance, to support our partners in the Western Balkans.

Conclusions

The fundamental condition to permanently overcome the current crisis is effective prevention of the further spread of COVID-19.

The majority of the recovery measures proposed in the EU will be financed from Next Generation EU programme, the financial resources of which are equal to EUR 750 billion. This solution constitutes a remarkable mechanism, which will enable many businesses to survive the crisis. Its financing will be possible, thanks to the decision on own resources, which in exceptional circumstances will allow the European Commission to apply for a loan of up to EUR 750 billion on the behalf of the EU. This will be feasible due to the bond issue and shall be purposed for the introduction of anti-crisis measures in the years 2021–2024. Consequently, the EU will ensure significant support to its Member States without exerting additional pressure on their already stretched national budgets.

Undoubtedly, the assessment of the degree to which the measures taken by the EU helped in the fight against the coronavirus as well as in overcoming the crisis will only be possible in time. At present, it is important to adapt the quantity and form of the support, both from the EU budget and national budgets of particular countries, to the constantly changing economic conditions as well as to react in due time, so that businesses can avoid bankruptcy and their employees can retain their jobs and sources of income.

Note

1 European instrument for temporary support aimed at mitigating unemployment risks in emergency situations.

References

Annexes to the Communication from the Commission to the European Parliament (2020). The European Council, the Council, the European Central Bank, the European Investment Bank and the Eurogroup. Brussels. Annex 3 – State Aid. https://eur-lex.europa.eu/legal-content/EN/TXT/?uri=CELEX:52020DC0112.

COM (2020). *Communication from the Commission. Coordinated Economic Response to the COVID-19 Outbreak, 112 Final.* Brussels: European Commission.

Conte, G. and Gualtieri, R. (2020). *Documento di Economia e Finanza 2020.* Roma: Ministero del Economia e Delle Finanze.

Coordinated Economic Response to the COVID-19 Outbreak (2020). *Communication from the European Commission, COM(2020) 112 Final.* Brussels.

Die Bundesregierung (2020). Leichterer Zugang zum Kurzarbeitergeld. https://www.bundesregierung.de/breg-de/themen/coronavirus/kurzarbeitergeld-1729626.

German Stability Programme (2020). Berlin: Federal Ministry of Finance. https://ec.europa.eu/info/sites/info/files/2020-european-stability-programme-germany_en.pdf.

Gesetz zur Errichtung eines Wirtschaftsstabilisierungsfonds (2020). *Wirtschaftsstabilisierungsfondsgesetz – WStFG.* Federal Ministry of Finance. https://www.bundesfinanzministerium.de/Web/EN/Home/home.html.

Grzeszak, J., Leśniewicz, F., Śliwowski, P. and Święcicki I. (2020). *Pandenomics. Zestaw narzędzi fiskalnych i monetarnych w dobie kryzysów.* Warszawa: Polski Instytut Ekonomiczny.

Key Instruments Supporting the Recovery Plan for Europe (2020). European Commission. https://ec.europa.eu/info/sites/info/files/factsheet_1_en.pdf.

Krzysztoszek, A. and Stam, C. (2020). *Francuski rząd przedstawia pakiet pomocowy dla krajowej gospodarki.* https://www.euractiv.pl/section/gospodarka/news/francja-rzad-pakiet-gospodarka-pandemia/.

Maślanka, Ł. (2020). Francuski plan odbudowy – 100 mld euro inwestycji w gospodarkę przyszłości. *Biuletyn Polskiego Instytutu Spraw Międzynarodowych 2020*, 188.

Overview of the Commission's Response, an Official Website of the European Union (2020). https://ec.europa.eu/info/live-work-travel-eu/health/coronavirus-response/recovery-plan-europe_en.

Pawłowski, M. (2020). Wpływ pandemii COVID-19 na politykę wewnętrzną i europejską Włoch. *Biuletyn PISM 2020*, 56.

Policy Measures Taken against the Spread and Impact of the Coronavirus (2020). Brussels: European Commission Directorate General Economic and Financial Affairs.

Recovery Plan for Europe, an Official Website of the European Union (2020). https://ec.europa.eu/info/live-work-travel-eu/health/coronavirus-response/recovery-plan-europe_en.

Śmigiel, M. and Łyjak, J. (2020). *Koronawirus a gospodarka UE Wpływ na wybrane kraje Unii Europejskiej.* Brussels: New Direction.

The EU Budget Powering the Recovery Plan for Europe (2020). European Commission. https://ec.europa.eu/info/sites/info/files/factsheet_1_en.pdf.

World Economic Outlook Database (2020). *Gross Domestic Product, Current Prices U.S. Dollars.* International Monetary Fund.

2 Stability of public finance in Poland and the EU before and during the COVID-19 pandemic

Janusz Kostecki

Introduction

Financial security, including security of the public finance sector, is one of the key factors that ensure the efficient functioning of the state and its sovereignty. Stability of the financial system is understood as: "... a state in which the financial system performs its functions in a continuous and effective manner, even in the event of unexpected and unfavorable circumstances and significant disturbances" (The National Bank of Poland, 2020).

In turn, the concept of stability of public finances was defined by the European Commission as:

> ...the government's ability to maintain in the long term the current level of its expenditure, tax policy and other related policies in such a way so as not to pose a threat to the solvency of the state and to fulfil all its financial obligations and approved expenditure.
>
> (EC, 2017)

The stability of public finances is regarded as a requirement to ensure sustainable socio-economic development and secure the state's position on the international arena.

Taking into account the requirements related to the security of public finances and maintaining or restoring their stability becomes of particular importance in times of economic and social challenges, such as those posed by the current pandemic.

The state of public finances in Poland, the European Union (EU), as well as in other countries around the world, in 2018–2020, was characterized by high volatility. The favourable economic circumstances since 2015 made it possible to increase public revenues and expenses in all sub-sectors of the state and local government institutions and to prevent their excessive imbalance. Any changes to that balance were to a large extent dictated by the current priorities of the socio-economic and fiscal policy, without sufficient consideration for the long-term goals. This prevented a significant improvement in the area of basic public services and support for innovative

DOI: 10.4324/9781003285717-2

sectors of the economy (Act of Parliament, 2009). The favourable economic situation came to an end in 2020. The main reason for the steep economic recession was the outbreak of the coronavirus pandemic at the end of 2019. The ongoing epidemiological crisis leads to the accumulation of numerous threats to the functioning of various aspects of the society and the economy, including the public finance system.

A reliable, albeit preliminary, assessment of the consequences of the existing social, economic and health difficulties for the state of the public finances in Poland and the EU requires the approach from a medium-term perspective, taking into account macroeconomic conditions. These conditions essentially determine the level of revenues and expenditure and the balance in the sphere of public finances, as well as have an impact on satisfying public needs.

Macroeconomic conditions of public finances in Poland and the EU in 2018–2020

The years 2018–2019 were a period of a favourable economic situation for Poland and was characterized by economic development, stability on the labour market, a moderate increase in the prices of consumer goods and services, as well as a slight slowdown in the growth rate of exports of goods and services. A significant economic downturn occurred in the second quarter of 2020, when gross domestic product (GDP) decreased by 8.4% compared to the corresponding period of the previous year (GUS, 2020; Table 2.1).

The real GDP growth rate in Poland in 2018 was one of the highest between 2010 and 2020, at 5.3%. It was 0.4% higher than in 2017 and exceeded the EU average for that period by as much as 3.3%. The main determinants of economic development were domestic demand and an increase in investment outlays, mainly in the general government sector. Compared to 2017, the former increased by 8.7%. In turn, the growth rate of the export of Polish goods and services, which previously stimulated the economy, has decreased in 2017–2018 from 9.5% to 6.5%. A slight deterioration of the situation in terms of international trade was characterized by a faster increase in imports than in exports and a negative balance of trade in goods and services.

In 2018, prices remained relatively stable. Inflation ran at 1.6%, which was at the lower limit of the inflation target set by the National Bank of Poland (2.5% +/− 1%). This was caused by favourable prices on the global markets for energy raw materials and agri-food products, as well as the balance on the domestic market of goods and services.

In 2019, Poland's GDP grew by 4.1%, which was higher than the value assumed in the budget. Compared to 2018, its growth rate decreased by 1.2%, but it was still higher than within the EU, the euro zone and in the global economy. The economic slowdown in 2019 was a consequence of the lower

Table 2.1 Real GDP growth rate and inflation rate in the EU in 2018–2021 [in %]

Countries/ regions	*GDP growth rate*				*Inflation rate*			
	2018	*2019*	*2020p*	*2021p*	*2018*	*2019*	*2020p*	*2021p*
EU-28/27	2.0	1.5	−8.3	5.6	1.9	1.5	0.6	1.3
Eurozone	1.8	1.3	−8.7	6.1	1.8	1.2	0.2	1.1
Belgium	1.5	1.4	−8.8	6.5	2.3	1.2	0.2	1.3
Bulgaria	3.1	3.4	−7.1	5.3	2.6	2.5	1.1	1.1
Czech Republic	3.2	2.3	−7.8	4.5	2.0	2.6	2.3	1.9
Denmark	2.4	2.3	−5.2	4.3	0.7	0.7	0.3	1.3
Germany	1.3	0.6	−6.3	5.3	1.9	1.4	0.3	1.4
Estonia	4.4	5.0	−7.7	6.2	2.4	2.3	0.7	1.7
Ireland	8.5	5.6	−8.5	6.3	0.7	0.9	−0.3	0.9
Greece	1.9	1.9	−9.0	6.0	0.8	0.5	−0.6	0.5
Spain	2.4	2.0	−10.9	7.1	1.7	0.8	0.0	1.0
France	1.8	1.5	−10.6	7.6	2.1	1.3	0.4	0.9
Croatia	2.7	2.9	−10.8	7.5	1.6	0.8	0.4	0.9
Italy	0.9	0.3	−11.2	6.1	1.2	0.6	−0.3	0.7
Cyprus	4.1	3.2	−7.7	5.3	0.8	0.5	−0.2	1.0
Latvia	4.3	2.2	−7.0	6.4	2.6	2.7	0.2	1.9
Lithuania	3.6	3.9	−7.1	6.7	2.5	2.2	0.8	1.5
Luxemburg	3.1	2.3	−6.2	5.4	2.0	1.6	0.7	1.6
Hungary	5.1	4.9	−7.0	6.0	2.9	3.4	3.0	2.7
Malta	5.2	4.9	−6.0	6.3	1.7	1.5	0.7	1.1
Netherlands	2.4	1.7	−6.8	4.6	1.6	2.7	0.8	1.3
Austria	2.4	1.6	−7.1	5.6	2.1	1.5	1.1	1.5
Poland	5.3	4.1	−4.4	4.3	1.2	2.1	2.5	2.8
Portugal	2.6	2.2	−9.8	6.0	1.2	0.3	−0.2	1.2
Romania	4.4	4.1	−6.0	4.0	4.1	3.9	2.5	3.1
Slovenia	4.1	2.4	−7.0	6.1	1.9	1.7	0.5	1.2
Slovakia	3.9	2.4	−9.0	7.4	2.5	2.8	1.9	1.1
Finland	1.5	1.1	6.3	2.8	1.2	1.1	0.5	1.4
Sweden	2.0	1.3	−5.3	3.1	2.0	1.7	0.4	1.1
UK[a]	1.3	1.5	−9.7	3.1	2.5	1.8	1.2	2.1

Source: Own study based on: Eurostat (2020); European Commission (2020).
p – Forecast of the European Commission (2020).
a As of February 1, 2020, Great Britain ceased to be a member of the European Union.

growth in domestic demand (by 2.6%) and capital accumulation, including investment in fixed assets by 2.2%. Protectionist tendencies in the world trade were also important and not without significance. The consequence of a reduced external demand was a slower growth rate of both exports and imports. The current account balance in relation to GDP was at the level of 0.5%, which was an increase compared to 2018 by 1.5%.

2019 brought an increase in inflation. According to the data of the Central Statistical Office, the inflation rate at the end of the year amounted to 2.3% (YoY), which was higher by 0.7% compared to inflation in 2018.

The situation on the labour market continued to improve. The unemployment rate at the end of 2019 was 5.2% and the continuing high demand for labour resulted in an increase in employment in the domestic economy and an increase by 8% in nominal wages.

The economic slowdown and the pandemic have forced a revision of the economic forecasts for the upcoming years. The European Commission estimates that in 2020 the growth rate of the Polish economy will drop to minus 4.4%, the unemployment rate will increase to 7.3%, while inflation will increase to 2.5%. The slowdown in economic activity will take a toll on both Polish companies and households. And while there are expectations that in 2021 the positive economic growth will be restored and GDP will increase by 4.3%, no signs of an end to the pandemic, with its second even more serious wave in the last quarter of 2020, indicate that in 2021 the economic situation, both in Poland and in other EU countries, may turn out to be worse than the optimistic expectations.

According to the International Monetary Fund (IMF), the GDP growth rate in the EU in the period 2018–2019 amounted to 2.3% and 1.7%, which placed the EU among the regions with lower dynamics of economic development (IMF, 2020). In turn, statistical data published by the European Commission and Eurostat indicate GDP growth lower by 0.2% (Table 2.1). The emerging and developing Asian countries, ASEAN-5 and Sub-Saharan Africa fared better in this regard than the EU. Nineteen Eurozone countries achieved poorer results for the EU as a whole. The economic growth rate of this group was 1.8% in 2018 and 1.3% in 2019. Diversification in this regard can be observed for individual EU Member States. In the analyzed period, the fastest growing economies were Ireland: 8.5% (2018) and 5.6% (2019), Poland: 5.3% (2018) and 4.1% (2019), and Romania: 4.4% (2018) and 4.1% (2019). The lowest economic growth rates were achieved by: Italy, Germany and Belgium. For neither of these countries, the annual real GDP growth rate exceeded 1.5%. What can also be observed regarding the economic situation in the EU countries is also a slowdown in economic activity by 1–2% in 2019, compared to the previous year.

Lack of major turmoil on the markets allowed the EU Member States to keep inflation within the limits set by the Maastricht fiscal criteria. The inflation rate, measured by the dynamics of consumer goods and services prices, ranged from 0.3% to 4.1%, with the lowest values for Cyprus, Denmark and Portugal, and the highest for Romania and Hungary (Table 2.1). Forecasts for 2020–2021 predict a further drop in inflation in 2020 (for some countries, deflation is expected), followed by its slight increase later on. The highest level (approx. 3%) is predicted for Romania and Poland.

The situation on the labour market in the analyzed period was less favourable. The average unemployment rate in the EU in 2018–2019 was approx. 7% (7.6% in the Eurozone). The current recession will drive the unemployment rate up by around 2% on average, with the most severe impact on countries such as Greece, Spain and Croatia.

Stability of the general government sector in Poland and the EU (according to the ESA 2010 methodology)

Public finances are defined as money resources at the disposal of the state and statutory organizations, as well as phenomena, streams and processes related to the accumulation of public funds and their distribution. Determination of the amount and structure of public funds and the effectiveness of their management requires to take into account many factors, including the use of appropriate methods for their measurement, analysis and evaluation (Jojko, 2008; Wernik, 2018). Both domestic and international standards and methodologies are used for this purpose. Taking into account domestic regulations (for Poland, it is mainly the Public Finance Act of 27 August 2009), allows for a more accurate and comprehensible interpretation and assessment of the functioning of the national public finance system, its sub-sectors and their units. On the other hand, international standards applied by individual states and international institutions are a reliable tool for comparison. EU Member States are required to send to the European Commission (Eurostat) the data on their fiscal situation, including the excessive deficit procedure (EDP). This obligation is imposed in the Council Regulation (EC) No 479/2009 of May 25, 2009, on the application of the Protocol on the EDP, annexed to the Treaty establishing the European Community. The required information is prepared in accordance with the methodology of the European System of National and Regional Accounts (ESA, 2010) and the Manual on Government Deficit and Debt adapted to it.

Revenues and expenditure of the general government sector

In accordance with the ESA 2010 standards, public finance is defined as the finance of the general government sector.

The revenues of this sector in Poland amounted to PLN 876.1 billion in 2018 and were higher than the revenues for the previous year by PLN 84.4 billion, i.e. by 10.7% (GUS, 2020).

The growth rate of public revenues was twice as high as the growth rate of GDP. As a result, the ratio of revenues of the analyzed sector to GDP increased from 39.8% to 41.3% (Table 2.2). The most marked increase in revenues was observed for the central government sub-sector, mostly from increased tax contributions related to production and import (by PLN 23.2 billion), social security contributions in the sub-sector of social welfare funds (by PLN 22.9 billion) and current taxes on income and property (by PLN 11.7 billion). The analysis of tax revenues points to the closing of tax gap, especially with regard to VAT. Previously, Poland was one of the EU Member States with the largest tax gap. In 2012–2015, it amounted to approx. 25%. In 2018, it was further reduced (by approx. PLN 25 billion) and reached the level of approx. 12.5%. Though the situation improved, there is still a need to take further measures in order to increase the efficiency of the tax collection system.

The increase in public revenues was accompanied by an increase in expenditure, which in 2018 amounted to PLN 881.2.1 billion and was PLN 60.0 billion (7.3%) higher than in the previous year. The general government expenditure ratio to GDP was 41.5% (0.2% higher than in 2017). The largest increase in expenditure was recorded for gross fixed capital formation, in particular in the local government institutions sub-sector (an increase by PLN 18.5 billion). This was partly due to the more intensive use of EU funds. A significant increase in expenditure was also related to social benefits (other than social transfers in kind) in the sub-sector of social security funds (an increase by PLN 14.6 billion – 6.3%). For several expenditure categories (e.g. subsidies and capital transfers), a decrease was recorded in the analyzed period.

The medium-term analysis of the period 2015–2018 shows a clear trend of a faster growth in total revenues than in total expenditure. During this period, the revenues increased by PLN 169.5 billion (by 24.2%), while the expenditure by PLN 128.8 billion (by 17.2%). This had a positive impact on the reduction of the negative balance of the general government sector, although it did not eventually lead to a surplus of revenues over expenditure.

The total revenues of the general government sector in 2019 amounted to PLN 941.0 billion and were by PLN 64.9 billion (7.4%) higher than the revenues for the previous year (GUS, 2020), mostly due to an increase in tax revenues and revenues from social security contributions (they represented 88% in the total increase in revenues). In turn, the expenditure of the analyzed sector amounted to PLN 956.9 billion, mostly on social benefits, wages and salaries and intermediate consumption. Investment expenditure accounted for 10.2% of the total expenditure and was quite low. The ratio of revenues and expenditure to GDP in 2019 was 41.1% and 41.8%, respectively.

The total GDP (in current prices) of the EU Member States in the years 2018 and 2019 amounted to EUR 15,938.8 billion and EUR 16,486.3 billion, respectively (Eurostat, 2020). Using the ratios of general government revenues and expenditure to GDP (Table 2.2), the amount of revenues and expenditures of the public finance sector was estimated. In 2018, the revenues of this sector amounted to EUR 7,188.4 billion, while expenditure to EUR 7,284.0 billion. In the following year, there was an increase in nominal GDP with a simultaneous slight decrease in revenues and an increase in expenditure. The nominal expenditure was EUR 7,418.8 billion, while the real expenditure amounted to EUR 7,550.7 billion. The presented figures show the scale of interventionism and the level of fiscalism in EU Member States.

In the period 2018–2019, the ratio of revenues to GDP in the EU was 45.0% for 2018 and 45.7% for 2019. The ratio of expenditure to GDP was slightly higher, at 45.0% in 2018 and 45.8% in 2019.

Table 2.2 General government revenues and expenditure in the EU in 2018–2019 [% of GDP]

Countries/regions	*Revenues*		*Expenditure*	
	2018	*2019*	*2018*	*2019*
UE-28	45.1	45.0	45.7	45.8
Eurozone-19	46.5	46.4	46.9	47.1
Belgium	51.4	50.1	52.2	52.1
Bulgaria	38.5	38.2	36.6	36.3
Czech Republic	41.5	41.6	40.6	41.3
Denmark	51.2	53.0	50.5	49.2
Germany	46.3	46.7	44.5	45.2
Estonia	38.7	39.0	39.2	38.9
Ireland	25.7	25.0	25.6	24.5
Greece	49.5	49.0	48.4	47.5
Spain	39.2	39.2	41.7	42.1
France	53.4	52.6	55.7	55.6
Croatia	46.3	47.4	46.0	47.0
Italy	46.2	47.0	48.4	48.6
Cyprus	39.5	41.5	43.0	40.1
Latvia	38.5	37.8	39.4	38.4
Lithuania	34.4	34.9	33.8	34.6
Luxemburg	45.3	44.6	42.2	42.2
Hungary	43.8	43.5	45.9	45.6
Malta	38.5	37.7	36.6	37.2
Netherlands	43.7	43.7	42.3	42.0
Austria	48.9	49.1	48.7	48.4
Poland	41.3	41.1	41.5	41.8
Portugal	42.9	42.7	43.2	42.7
Romania	31.9	31.8	34.9	36.1
Slovenia	44.3	43.8	43.5	43.3
Slovakia	40.7	41.4	41.7	42.7
Finland	52.5	52.3	53.4	53.3
Sweden	50.7	49.9	49.8	49.4
UK	38.8	38.8	41.1	41.1

Source: Own elaboration based on: Eurostat (2020); European Commission (2020).

The importance of the general government finance sector in meeting the needs of EU citizens and the efficient functioning of the economy varies for individual EU Member States. Eurostat data indicates that for most EU countries, the ratio of total general government revenues to GDP fluctuates around the average value for this group. In 2019, this value slightly exceeded 50% in four countries, while in nine it was below 40%. It is worth to mention Ireland and Romania, as in these two countries, the burden on the economy as a source of financing public needs is relatively low and in 2019 amounted to 24.5% and 36.1%, respectively. The level of expenditure is essentially correlated with the level of revenues, with the deviations in plus or in minus. The former was true for 14 countries where the revenues to GDP ratio was higher than that of expenditure for two consecutive years before the pandemic. Medium-term surplus of revenues over expenditure does not necessarily indicate a good condition of the economy and the public finance sector, as it may be due to the implementation of recovery measures to combat excessive debt, as was the case in Greece.

The results of the public finance sector and public debt as determinants of public finance stability

The public finance sector is considered to be sustainable when its financial results do not show a deficit of revenues in relation to expenditure, and the process of public debt management is quite smooth (Moździerz, 2009). Although imbalance in this regard is observed in many countries, it does not always mean the loss of financial stability and the ability to perform functions and tasks assigned to public sector entities: central and local government units and social security institutions. The permissible deviations from the state of balance can be justified both by the theory of public finance (e.g. the theory of impasse, the theory of cyclical equilibrium, the concept of operation above/below the line), the socio-economic strategy and policy as well as budget practices (Gaudemet, Molinier, 2000). When determining the scope of permissible deviations from the state of sustainability of the finance sector, international economic organizations (e.g. the IMF, EBRD, EU) as well as the competent institutions of individual countries negatively assess the presence of significant budget deficits and excessive financial obligations that may not be fulfilled.

In the analysis of the condition of the public finance sector in the EU, particular attention is paid to issues related to its balance and indebtedness. This is due to the fact that the results of the public finance sector and public debt are one of the criteria for assessing the security and financial stability of individual EU Member States. These are the so-called Maastricht fiscal criteria applicable to the general government sector. According to the criteria, the ratio of the annual general government deficit relative to GDP must not exceed 3%, while the ratio of gross government debt relative to GDP must not exceed 60%.

From the point of view of financial balance, the situation of the general government sector in Poland, as well as in most EU countries in the period 2018–2019, should be considered as relatively stable, although experiencing certain difficulties. A significant deterioration was observed in 2020 due to the outbreak of the COVID-19 pandemic and the deepening economic recession, the consequences of which will be experienced for the next several or even more years.

In terms of the results of the general government sector in recent years, what can be noticed is a decrease in the ratio of the public finance deficit to GDP, with the simultaneous increase in nominal debt and its decrease in the ratio to GDP.

In 2018, the Polish general government sector recorded a deficit of PLN 5.1 billion. In relation to GDP, it amounted to PLN 2,121.6 billion (0.2%)

(GUS, 2020). This result was much better than the result in the previous year, when the budget deficit amounted to PLN 29.6 billion (1.5% of GDP). The total general government deficit in 2018 was calculated on the basis of (MF, 2019a, b):

- the deficit of the central government sub-sector (mainly the budget) in the amount of PLN 11.7 billion (0.5% of GDP). The reduction in the deficit of this sub-sector compared to 2017 amounted to as much as PLN 60.9 billion (2.9% of GDP),
- the surplus of the social security funds sub-sector in the amount of PLN 13.7 billion (0.6% of GDP),
- the deficit of the local government sector in the amount of PLN 6.7 billion (0.3% of GDP). Compared to 2017, the results of this sub-sector were down by PLN 7.8 billion.
- In the medium-term perspective, for the period 2014–2018, Poland reduced the deficit of the analyzed sector by 2.2%.

The year 2019 brought a deterioration of the situation, though there was no danger of failure to meet the standards established by the Maastricht fiscal criteria. Although the result of the analyzed sector showed significant volatility for individual quarters of the year, at the end of the budget year, the deficit amounted to PLN 15.9 billion (0.7% of GDP) (GUS, 2020). The amount was a consequence of the more than twofold increase in the deficit of the central government sub-sector. The sub-sector of local government institutions recorded a much smaller deficit of PLN 4.7 billion (0.2% of GDP). The social security funds sub-sector achieved a budget surplus, which was similar to the result for 2018 (PLN 13.7 billion, 0.6% of GDP).

When assessing the results of the Polish general government sector in the period 2008–2019, a certain progress is observed. In 2008–2014, the deficit of this sector exceeded 3% in relation to GDP, which resulted in the launching of the excessive deficit procedure by the European Commission. The year 2015 turned out to be a breakthrough year, when the deficit dropped to 2.6% and continued to decrease in the following years. The favourable trend was stopped by the outbreak of the COVID-19 pandemic and its negative consequences. The forecasts for 2020 indicate a high probability of a deficit of 9.5%, which is expected to decrease to 4.5% in the following year. This, however, may prove difficult in view of the deepening recession.

The situation of the Polish general government sector showed many similarities to the tendencies observed for the public finance sector in the vast majority of EU countries. In the last few years before the recession, the imbalance between revenues and expenditure was reduced both in the EU and in the Eurozone. This is evidenced by the low level of the deficit in relation to GDP in the EU-28, which in the period 2018–2019 amounted to 0.7% for 2018 and 0.8% for 2019, while in the Eurozone: 0.5% for 2018 and 0.6% for 2019 (Table 2.2). The relatively favourable economic circumstances and

Table 2.3 Surplus/deficit and consolidated general government debt in the EU in 2008–2021 [% of GDP]

Countries/regions	*Surplus/deficit*				*Public debt*			
	2018	*2019*	*2020p*	*2021p*	*2018*	*2019*	*2020p*	*2021p*
UE-28	−0.4	−0.6	−8.3	−3.6	81.3	79.4	95.1	92.0
Eurozone-19	−0.5	−0.6	−8.5	−3.5	87.8	86.0	102.7	98.8
Belgium	−0.8	−1.9	−8.9	−4.2	99.8	98.6	113.8	110.0
Bulgaria	2.0	2.1	−2.8	−1.8	22.3	20.4	25.5	25.4
Czech Republic	0.9	0.3	−6.7	−4.0	32.6	30.8	38.7	39.9
Denmark	0.7	3.7	−7.2	−2.3	33.9	33.2	44.7	44.6
Germany	1.9	1.4	−7.0	−1.5	61.9	59.8	75.7	71.8
Estonia	−0.6	−0.3	−8.3	−3.4	8.4	8.4	20.7	22.6
Ireland	0.1	0.4	−5.6	−2.9	63.5	58.8	66.4	66.7
Greece	1.0	1.5	−6.4	−2.1	181.2	176.6	196.4	182.6
Spain	−2.5	−2.8	−10.1	−6.7	97.6	95.5	115.6	113.7
France	−2.3	−3.0	−9.9	−4.0	98.1	98.1	116.5	111.9
Croatia	0.2	0.4	−7.1	−2.2	74.7	73.2	88.6	83.4
Italy	−2.2	−1.6	−11.1	−5.6	134.8	134.8	158.9	153.6
Cyprus	−3.7	1.7	−7.0	−1.8	100.6	95.5	115.7	105.0
Latvia	−0.8	−0.2	−7.3	−4.5	37.2	36.9	43.1	43.7
Lithuania	0.6	0.3	−6.9	−2.7	33.8	36.3	48.5	48.4
Luxemburg	3.1	2.2	−4.8	0.1	21.0	22.1	26.4	25.7
Hungary	−2.1	−2.0	−5.2	−4.0	70.2	66.3	75.0	73.5
Malta	1.9	0.5	−6.7	−2.5	45.6	43.1	50.7	50.8
Netherlands	1.4	1.7	−6.3	−3.5	52.4	48.6	62.1	57.6
Austria	0.2	0.7	−6.1	−1.9	74.0	70.4	78.8	75.8
Poland	−0.2	−0.7	−9.5	−3.8	48.8	46.0	58.5	58.3
Portugal	−0.4	0.2	−6.5	−1.8	122	117.7	131.6	124.4
Romania	−2.9	−4.3	−9.2	−11.4	34.7	35.2	46.2	54.7
Slovenia	0.7	0.5	−7.2	−2.1	70.4	66.1	83.7	79.9
Slovakia	−1.0	−1.3	−8.5	−4.2	49.4	48.0	59.5	59.9
Finland	−0.9	−1.1	−7.4	−3.4	59.6	59.4	69.4	69.6
Sweden	0.8	0.5	−5.6	−2.2	38.8	35.1	42.6	42.5
UK	−2.2	−2.1	−10.5	−6.7	85.7	85.4	102.1	101.5

Source: Own elaboration based on: Eurostat (2020); European Commission (2020).
p – Forecast of the European Commission (2020).

prudent fiscal policy allowed 14 Member States to obtain a budget surplus, which was most pronounced in Bulgaria, Denmark and the Netherlands. The remaining countries (except for Cyprus in 2018) showed a general government deficit of less than 3% in relation to GDP. Its highest level was in Romania, France and Spain.

The macroeconomic situation of Poland and other EU Member States with a budget deficit should encourage planning sustainable budgets and reducing public debt, which in the longer term will allow to reduce the costs of its management and rationalize public expenditure (Onofrei, Tofan, Vatamanu, 2020). This, however, was unfortunately not the case.

Sliding of the economies of EU Member States into a deep recession in 2020 forced a rapid increase in public expenditure related to healthcare and financing programmes supporting the functioning of economic entities, both in the public and private sectors. At the same time, a significant slowdown in economic activity resulted in a decrease in public revenues. This generated an unprecedented increase in general government finance deficits. The projected budget deficit, estimated for the EU, is expected to amount to 8.3% in 2020 and 3.6% in 2021 (Table 2.3). The highest budget deficits in 2020 are expected for the following countries: Italy (11.1%), Spain (10.1%), France (9.9%) and Poland (9.5%), and possibly – Romania (Bostan, Toderascu, Gavriluta, 2018). The main method of financing the deficits was incurring by the state and statutory institutions liabilities on domestic and international financial markets.

In terms of ensuring the security and stability of the public finance sector, the amount and structure of public debt is of great importance. Both in the theory of public debt and in the strategy of its management, there are various assessment methodologies. Taking into account the EU and Polish public debt methodologies, three main types of public debt can be distinguished: public debt, State Treasury debt and public debt of general government institutions. There is also what is called a hidden public debt (GUS, 2015). Conducting reliable analyses and comparison with other countries enables the use of data on debt related to the finances of the general government sector.

The debt of the general government sector in Poland at the end of 2018 amounted to PLN 1,035.7 billion (GUS, 2020). Compared to the previous year, a nominal increase of PLN 28.5 billion (2.8%) was recorded. With a GDP growth of 5.1%, the ratio of the debt of this sector to GDP decreased from 50.6% in 2017 to 48.8% in 2018 (Table 2.3). Poland's public debt in 2018, calculated according to ESA 2010, was therefore PLN 50.1 billion lower, and its relation to GDP decreased by 2%.

The increase in the general government debt was also recorded in 2019 (MF, 2020a, c) and amounted to PLN 1,045.1 billion. Compared to 2018, this represents an increase by PLN 9.4 billion (0.9%). At the same time, it was PLN 54.2 billion higher than the public debt after consolidation, calculated according to the domestic methodology. The calculated growth rate of the general government debt in 2019 was by 3.2% lower than the GDP growth rate, which means a decrease in relation to GDP. At the end of December 2019, the debt to GDP ratio was 46.0% and was 2.8% lower than the ratio at the end of 2018.

The total debt of the general government sector at the end of 2019 was made up of the debt incurred by:

- the central government sub-sector – PLN 956.8 billion,
- the local government sub-sector – PLN 88.4 billion.

The social security fund sub-sector did not record a deficit. The State Treasury had the largest share in the general government debt.

The total debt of the Polish general government sector was much lower compared to the average results in the EU and the Eurozone in 2018–2019.

Forecasts expect a rapid increase in public debt in 2020–2021. Its relation to GDP is estimated to amount to 58.5% in 2020 and 58.3% in 2021 (Table 2.3). Somewhat higher ratios are predicted by the Polish Ministry of Finance (61.9% and 64.1%, respectively). The nominal value of debt at the end of 2020 is estimated at PLN 1,384.0 billion (MF, 2020b). The above-mentioned trend is corroborated by the amount of general government debt at the end of the second quarter of 2020, when it reached PLN 1,256.0 billion (an increase by PLN 210.9 billion – 20.2% in the first year of the pandemic). Such a significant increase in public debt in such a short period of time has been observed for the first time in the last three decades.

At the end of 2018, the average general government debt to GDP ratio in the EU was 81.3% and in the Eurozone 87.8% (Table 2.3). This value is quite high, well above 60%, which is considered acceptable in the Maastricht fiscal criteria. The year 2019 brought a slight improvement and the analyzed ratio dropped by 1.9% and 1.8%, respectively. In 2019, particularly high level of debt (exceeding 100% of GDP) was recorded in such countries as Greece, Italy, Portugal, France, France, Spain, the United Kingdom and Cyprus. On the other hand, in sixteen EU Member States, the level of debt did not significantly affect their financial stability. The lowest general government debt to GDP ratio was recorded in Estonia (8.4%), Bulgaria (20.4%) and Luxembourg (22.1%).

According to the forecasts for 2020, all EU Member States are likely to record an increase in the public finance debt, both in nominal and relative terms. Depending on the country, it will amount to several or as much as over 20% in relation to GDP. This will undermine financial security and its restoration will require considerable efforts by individual countries, enterprises and households in the years to come.

Conclusions

The analysis of the financial situation in the general government sector in Poland and the EU in 2018–2020 showed its relatively good condition in the first two years of the analyzed period and a significant deterioration in 2020. Most EU countries did not take advantage of the period of good economic situation and significant public revenues to strengthen or restore the sustainability of the public finance sector. The fiscal policy of many countries favoured current political and social goals. Less importance was attached to making strategic decisions and systemic changes that would enable lasting and noticeable improvements in the field of public services, including health protection, social welfare, education, environmental protection or retirement and disability insurance. The support from the public finance sector for ensuring scientific development, innovation of enterprises and competitiveness of the economy is still insufficient.

During the period of economic recession caused by the COVID-19 pandemic and the slowdown in economic activity, the public finance sector has become an important source of financing for domestic and international anti-crisis and health protection programmes. Due to the lack of budget reserves, the required funds are obtained by incurring significant public liabilities and increasing the public debt. There is a famous Polish proverb, which says: "No time to grieve for roses when the forests are burning", which is a good reflection of the current situation. In this case, the roses represent the public finance sector that must be sacrificed to save the economy and protect people's health.

The reflections and observations presented in this chapter also allow to formulate the following conclusions:

- fiscal policy should be characterized by equilibrium, taking into account political, financial, environmental and health aspects;
- risk management and preparedness for crises, regardless of their cause (economic, climate, health, etc.) should be considered an important element of the public finance management strategy;
- individual countries and the EU need to create budget reserves in the general government sector, regardless of the current state of the balance of revenues and expenditure. Such reserves should amount to approx. 8–10% of annual revenues;
- it is important to stop treating general government debt management as an intergenerational liability and to adopt prudence procedures.

References

Act of Parliament (2009). *Ustawa o finansach publicznych z dnia 27 sierpnia 2009 r.* Warsaw: Internetowy System Aktów Prawnych.

Bostan, I., Toderascu, C. and Gavriluta, A.F. (2018). Public Finance Sustainability in Romania – Challenges and Vulnerabilities. *Preprints*, 2018070461.

ESA (2010). *Rozporządzenie Parlamentu Europejskiego i Rady (UE) nr 549/2013 z dnia 21 maja 2013 r.* https://stat.gov.pl/obszary-tematyczne/rachunki-narodowe/europejski-zystem-rachunkow-narodowych-i-regionalnych-esa-2010/rozporzadzenie-parlamentu-europejskiego-i-rady-ue-nr-5492013-z-dnia-21-maja-2013-r-, 1,1.html.

European Commission (2017). *Europejski semestr – zestawienie informacji tematycznych. Stabilność finansów publicznych*, 1–18. https://ec.europa.eu/info/sites/info...public-finance-sustainability_pl.pdf.

European Commission (2020). *Main Economic Indicators 2011-2021.* https://ec.europa.eu/poland/sites/poland/files/docs/news/2020_sef_tables_en.pdf.

Eurostat (2020). https://ec.europa.eu/eurostat/data/database.

Gaudemet, P.J. and Molinier, J. (2000). *Finanse publiczne.* Warsaw: PWE.

GUS (2015). *Uprawnienia emerytalno-rentowe gospodarstw domowych nabyte w ramach ubezpieczeń społecznych według stanu na dzień 31 grudnia 2015 r.* https://stat.gov.pl/obszary-tematyczne/rachunki-narodowe/nabyte-uprawnienia-emerytalno-rentowe-w-ramach-ubezpieczen-spolecznych/uprawnienia-

emerytalno-rentowe-gospodarstw-domowych-nabyte-w-ramach-ubezpieczen-spolecznych-wedlug-stanu-na-dzien-31-grudnia-2015-r-, 1,1.html.
GUS (2020). *Komunikat dotyczący deficytu i długu sektora instytucji rządowych i samorządowych w 2019 r.*, 1–4. https://stat.gov.pl/obszary-tematyczne/rachunki-narodowe/statystyka-sektora-instytucji-rzadowych-i-samorzadowych/komunikat-dotyczacy-deficytu-i-dlugu-sektora-instytucji-rzadowych-i-samorzadowych-w-2019-r-, 1,30.html.
IMF (2020). *World Economic Database.* https://www.imf.org/en/Publications/WEO/weo-database/2020/October/select-subjects?a=1&c=001.
Jojko, B. (2008). *Dług publiczny a równowaga fiskalna.* Warsaw: CeDeWu.
MF (2019a). *Informacja kwartalna o stanie finansów publicznych w IV kwartale 2018 r. i w całym 2018 r., 2/2019*, 1–17. https://www.gov.pl/web/finanse/informacja-kwartalna-o-stanie-finansow-publicznych-w-iv-kwartale-2018-r-i-calym-2018-r.
MF (2019b). *Zadłużenie Sektora Finansów Publicznych IV kw./2018. Biuletyn kwartalny, 29.03.2019 r.*, 1–7. https://www.gov.pl/attachment/473d4465-dec3-4bc1-a2e0-077f37785c53.
MF (2020a). *Informacja kwartalna o stanie finansów publicznych w II kwartale 2020 r., 4/2020*, 1–36. https://www.gov.pl/web/finanse/informacja-kwartalna-o-stanie-finansow-publicznych-w-ii-kwartale-2020-r.
MF (2020b). *Strategia zarządzania długiem sektora finansów publicznych w latach 2021-2024.* Warsaw: Ministerstwo Finansów. https://www.gov.pl/web/finanse/strategie-zarzadzania-długiem.
MF (2020c). *Zadłużenie Sektora Finansów Publicznych IV kw./2019. Biuletyn kwartalny, 31.03.2020 r.*, 1–7. https://www.gov.pl/attachment/6ba6d26f-c84b-41e2-be9e-3ad96baeec40.
Moździerz, A. (2009). *Nierównowaga finansów publicznych.* Warsaw: PWE.
NBP (2020). *Raport o stabilności systemu finansowego.* https://www.nbp.pl/home.aspx?f=/systemfinansowy/stabilnosc.html.
Onofrei, M., Tofan, M. and Vatamanu, A.F. (2020). Fiscal Responsibility Legal Framework – New Paradigm for Fiscal Discipline in the EU. *Risks*, 8(3), 79.
Wernik, A. (2018). Finanse publiczne w 20017 roku – próba analizy. *Zeszyty naukowe Uczelni Vistula. Ekonomia*, XVII, 63(6), 9–23.

3 Disinformation of the digital era revolution in conditions of COVID-19

Wiesława Załoga and Robert Maciejczyk

Introduction

The advancement of computer technology, the Internet and new communication platforms over the past two decades have revolutionized the way we create, exchange and respond to information. The growing role of the Internet as the main source of gaining news about the world has made articles in newspapers and weekly magazines more and more important to the public debate, but comments on portals, social media profiles, videoblogs or emotional selfies.

In recent years, the world public opinion has also learned about the existence of phenomena that cause a number of controversies. New tools for influencing social views and emotions are used today not only by competing parties and politicians, but also by private persons, influential companies, non-governmental and international organizations or governments and special services of foreign countries. The effectiveness of these activities depends primarily on the level of media competence and social awareness of the problem among citizens.

The prevailing perception is that the increased presence of fake news poses a challenge to our democratic society. Therefore, we try to understand and identify the security gap in the media environment in order to limit the phenomenon and consequences of fake news. The appropriate level of knowledge and situational awareness in the field of security in the virtual world and ongoing research in many environments seem to be useful in combating fake news. By identifying a gap in our knowledge of how to respond to fake news, as well as the potential for technological innovation and future lines of research to fill these gaps, we can try to limit the negative effects of false information on public opinion. The biggest challenge may be not only to establish effective mechanisms to counter fake news, but rather how to implement them without undermining the institutions that are essential to maintaining a democratic system.

Fake news actions by government bodies primarily involve two types of action. First, it focuses on implementing procedures, regulations or laws aimed at reducing the spread of false information. Second, it aims to support

DOI: 10.4324/9781003285717-3

institutions or entities responsible for coordinating national activities aimed at raising awareness and raising public awareness of the impact of fake news on public opinion. These are activities that are constantly subject to constant changes and improvements dictated by the requirements of the market supported by modern technology.

> With the increase in disinformation activities related to the Covid-19 pandemic, European Union (EU) institutions are trying to disseminate knowledge about the dangers of disinformation and encourage the use of reliable sources. The EU also turned to online platforms to help tackle fake news and other misinformation and remove illegal or false content. In this way, more than 3.4 million suspicious Twitter accounts participating in the discussions have been detected since the start of the pandemic about the Covid-19 pandemic.
>
> (Consilium Europa, 2020)

The participation of disinformation in the manipulation of social consciousness

One of the most common methods of manipulation in the media is information distortion and disinformation. Transforming the original message into a more general or more specific one, taking words out of context to assign a different function to statements and falsifying the message to create content that is contrary to the original are the most common ways of misleading recipients (Fallis, 2015).

The problem of manipulating information is a common phenomenon, we deal with it on a daily basis in various situations. Currently, the media have the largest share in manipulating information. Most often, we encounter manifestations of manipulation or persuasion using television, the Internet, press, radio or various types of advertising, e.g. on the street, in a shop, etc.

Manipulation is a process consisting of a specific sequence of treatments, which makes it easier to influence someone else's decisions. Manipulating information is therefore a process performed on the flow of information from the sender to the recipient. As for the transmission of information, they may include omitting certain information, suggesting information by the order in which it is presented, lying or even fraudulent provision of information. Media manipulation with the use of psychosocial techniques has become a very dangerous weapon in the fight against patriotism, identity and European values (Batorowska, Klepka, Wasiuta, 2019, p. 263).

On June 10, 2020, the European Commission and the High Representative for Foreign Affairs and Security Policy issued a joint communiqué entitled "Fight with Covid-19 misinformation – we are giving the facts a voice". Among other things, they proposed how to concretely increase the EU's resilience to disinformation. They indicated the need to step up EU support for scientists and fact-checkers, strengthen EU strategic communication and increase cooperation with international partners, while promoting freedom of expression and pluralism (www.consilium.europa.eu/pl/policies/coronavirus/fighting-disinformation). The problem of manipulation in the network is noticed not only by international organizations, companies operating on an international scale or representatives of non-governmental organizations, but also by ordinary Internet users. Due to the transnational nature of the Internet, there are currently no entities that can tackle these challenges alone. For this reason, media competences of recipients and social awareness of the problem are so important.

Disinformation and imposing emotional perception of reality serve the purpose of the aggressor. The lack of control over manipulation is most often associated with the subject's lack of knowledge about this phenomenon and the awareness of being manipulated (Wasiuta, Wasiuta, 2018).

A key element in how we consume information is trust in the sources it comes from. The Internet, as the newest and most accessible mass medium in terms of ease of publication, is characterized by other elements that build trust between the sender and the recipient than, for example, television or radio. The respondents were asked a number of questions concerning selected aspects of trust in the contemporary phenomena in digital media.

Disinformation is the deliberate creation and dissemination of false or manipulated information intended to deceive and mislead the public, either for the purpose of harming or for political, personal or financial gain (Design102, 2019).

When the information environment is deliberately manipulated, it can (Design102, 2019):

- threaten public safety;
- break community cohesion;
- reduce trust in institutions and the media;
- weaken public acceptance of science's role in communicating policy development and implementation;
- harm our economic well-being and our global influence;
- undermine the integrity of the government, constitution and our democratic process.

Disinformation is about exerting influence. People who disseminate don't want people to make conscious, sensible choices. They try to accomplish by deliberately shortening the usual decision-making processes. The basic techniques are simple – we call them the First Principles of Disinformation (Design102, 2019):

Fake photos manipulate the content, e.g. a forged document or image in Photoshop (Design102, 2019):

- conceals identity or falsely assigns source: for example, fake social media account or scammer;

- the rhetoric uses malicious or false arguments: for example, for trolls agitating commentators in the chat forum;
- symbolism uses events to value their communication: for example, terrorist attacks;
- technology takes advantage of technological advantage: sample bots automatically amplify messages.

The principles of disinformation are often combined to have a greater impact on the social environment.

Misinformation is the manipulation of information that is intentionally misleading and deceiving, while disinformation is inaccurate information that is the result of honest error or neglect. During the hearing on the Kremlin's propaganda efforts, the chairman of the US House of Representatives of the Foreign Affairs Committee, Ed Royce, warned that information manipulation by Russia "may be more dangerous than any military, as no artillery can stop their lies from spreading and undermining U.S. security interests in Europe" (McGreal, 2020).

Disinformation as a systemic tool is a modern invention of mankind than propaganda. Disinformation is strong appeal to the emotions of a large number of people; promoting not real, but an imaginary virtual object, which actively breaks the usual image of the world; something that cannot be refuted, because it is difficult to do in the case of non-existent objects – e.g. Russian official news agencies in the first period of the war with Ukraine called the Ukrainian government a junta, and the armed forces called butchers, choosing terms repeatedly used in the past with the most negative connotations (Batorowska, Klepka, Wasiuta, 2019).

Forms of disinformation and manipulation

The basic ways of creating biased information include unverifiable non-truthfulness, confusing truth with falsehood (e.g. misinformation through titles), distorting the truth (false objectivity), modifying context, blurring, selecting facts, guiding commentary, illustration, generalization, unequal proportions (e.g. some provocation resulted in police repression; a large publication on repression will be included, and only mention is made of provocation), equal proportions (e.g. for assessing a fact two equally long opinions are given, but one is brilliant, factual and convincing, and the second – chaotic, hardly understood). Plus: complete omission of facts, biased poll, deceptive presentation of statistics.

In the face of the constantly increasing flow of information, or rather disinformation, the selection of messages that are relevant, informative, useful, credible and up-to-date and at the same time objective, as opposed to those that can be a tool of manipulation, becomes more and more difficult for the average person to perform. It becomes clear that the problem of disinformation does not only concern the average person, but also, for example, corporate environments making key business decisions. The problem affects all of us and causes a feeling of helplessness and powerlessness in the face of the information flood.

One way an attempt is made to penetrate public consciousness is through the activity of "trolls" (bogus Internet accounts) and "bots" (accounts operated by automated processes). These establish direct contact with readers of various media around the world (Lawrence, 2020).

"Troll farms", which offer the service of "renting" a large number of active social media accounts, "fake news" or content pretending to be reliable journalism, micro-targeting, often based on violating the privacy of users, user profiling or trolling, which usually refers to pseudo-anonymous attacks on social environments. These are some of the phenomena that have triggered discussions and polemics in recent years.

In an interview with Radio Free Europe (RFE), a former Russian troll revealed how "thousands of fake Twitter, Facebook, LiveJournal and vKontakte accounts" were created to uphold and promote Moscow's position on several issues, and to create the impression of a plurality of opinions in the information space (Volchek, Sindelar, 2020).

The wider activity of troll factories includes the use of blogs, false stories and opinions in articles posted on pseudo-news sites. By increasing the flow of information and artificially creating the impression of diversity of opinion in the information space, trolling inevitably weakens the readers' ability to discern opinions and messages, which further deceive global audiences in their search for objective truth. The very nature of the global Internet space makes effectively inserting disinformation into respected media much easier and cheaper than ever before, which is beneficial to hostile environment efforts to create a free environment (Averin, 2018).

In carrying out the research project, respondents were invited to participate in a study on disinformation online in a crisis situation affecting state security. The respondents were asked to assess, based on their own experiences, which forms of disinformation or manipulation they most often experienced in the last six months? The research results are presented graphically in Chart 3.1.

Based on their personal experiences, the participants of the study assessed that they most often dealt with forms of disinformation and manipulation in cyberspace in the form of false news. Analyzing the scientific research described in the literature of the latest publications, this opinion is often confirmed. In this study, this form obtained the highest rate, as much as 31.19%. The respondents who indicated a form of disinformation trolling, 19.12% were in second place. The answer that may indicate a low level of awareness of the respondents about the existence or distinction between forms of manipulation and disinformation was placed in third place. In this case, the answer was: it is difficult to say what constitutes 17.54% of the answers. The high rate of 14.30% indicated false photos.

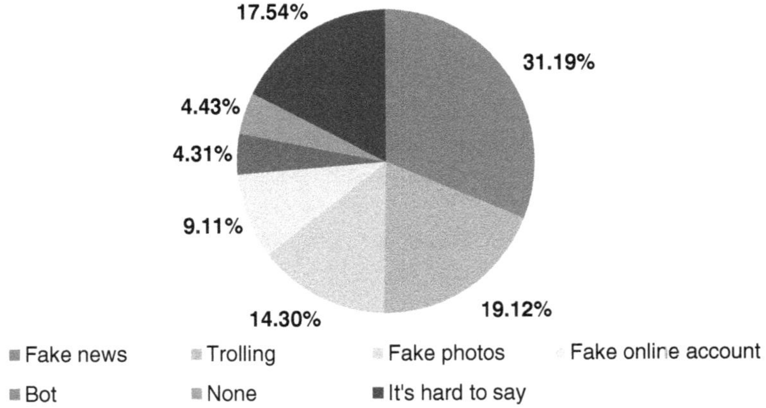

Chart 3.1 Percentage distribution of responses to the question: Based on the respondents' experiences over the past six months, which of the following forms of disinformation or manipulation did they most often experience?

Source: Own elaboration.

The presented research results prove the need to build awareness of the society in the field of information security. It is a necessity dictated by the massive influx of false information in every social environment. The COVID-19 pandemic is conducive to undesirable behavior in an aggressive information policy on a global scale. When analyzing the results of the research, it can be argued that the society is better educated and uses the media better than ever before. However, society requires shaping and building the development of social awareness, and thanks to this attitude we will shape and build resistance to propaganda and disinformation.

Social awareness in the area of media disinformation

Disinformation, regardless of the entity involved in the activity, by definition creates aggressive marketing in an attempt to achieve the assumed goals and introduce social anxiety by misleading the social environment. Such aggressive actions can lead to damage which in a democratic environment can be irreversible. In order to test and diagnose the level of trust in the content published on the Internet, the respondents were asked: how often do they come across information on the Internet that they consider falsified or manipulated? The analysis of the results of the conducted study is presented graphically in Chart 3.2.

From the presented research results, we can conclude that the respondents are not aware of the existence of false information and the situation of disinformation at the appropriate level. To the question: how often do respondents find information on the Internet that they believe to be falsified

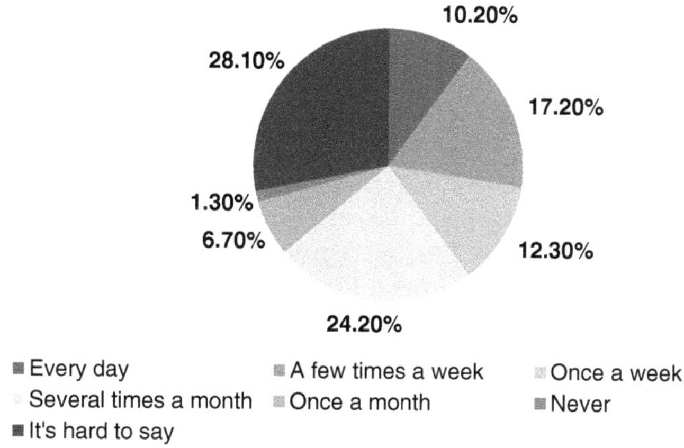

Chart 3.2 Percentage distribution of answers to the question: how often do respondents come across information on the Internet that they believe was falsified or manipulated?
Source: Own elaboration.

or manipulated? The responses were as follows: a high rate of 28.10% proves the lack of awareness of the society as a result of the conducted research. The next group constitutes 24.20% of respondents who assessed that they encounter falsified information several times a month, 17.20% of respondents several times a week, and 12.30% once a week. Taking into account the highest indicator, which proves the lack of awareness and knowledge of the society about the scale of false information in the virtual world, it can be assumed that after making respondents aware of the risk of obtaining false information online, the research results may change significantly.

It is not surprising that the Internet as the main medium of information today is not generally trusted by Internet users. Analyzing the results of research as part of the project on disinformation in the network in a crisis situation affecting the state security, the results show that a large percentage of respondents (averaging about 50%) trust information published on the Internet, while the experience of recent months during the COVID-19 pandemic makes over 30% of adult Internet users say that information on the Internet is falsified. The experiences of manipulating and falsifying content mean that, according to the respondents, traditional media such as the press, television or radio are the least exposed to spreading, for example, fake news.

Contemporary techniques of Internet manipulation are often invisible to outside observers, they can be observed primarily through data flow analyses within the information infrastructure of the network, in particular in social media. At the same time, the level of protection of citizens against disinformation depends to a large extent on the awareness of the problem among recipients. Data analysis made it possible to distinguish three social groups that check the credibility of information. The first group refers to "personal trust dictated by the fact that: the author is a person whom the respondent trusts or is published or recommended by someone whom the respondent knows, and that he or she comes from a medium the respondent trusts". The second group that emerged from the study was that of journalistic integrity. The main assumptions of the selected group are that the information contains different points of view and that it contains information about sources. The third group of respondents represents the position of social proof of rightness. This means, for example, that information is communicated by many people or media simultaneously and that it comes from a large or popular medium. The assessment of the authenticity of content on the web determines the practices of Internet users who were asked whether they checked the credibility of content, sources, authors or profiles while using the Internet during the pandemic. Chart 3.3 presented below shows the percentage distribution of answers to the question about verifying the credibility of individual elements of content posted on the Internet.

The research question asked the respondents concerned the most important factors for the respondents, which are taken into account when assessing the credibility of information in the cyberspace environment. The data analysis illustrated in the presented charts allows for drawing far-reaching conclusions. The first conclusion concerns the credibility of the content of information posted on the Internet, where Internet users constitute a group of only 23.07%. This is, contrary to the expectations of the researchers, an indicator which suggests, however, that the respondents do not always check the sources from which they obtained information. A total of 20.40% of respondents trust the media they trust. Another group of 18.12% analyzes the obtained information from different points of view. The public also gets information signed by authors they trust. In this case, the respondents constitute 16.03% of the respondents.

When looking for a form of defense against manipulation of information posted on the web, respondents consciously set credibility attributes for the content they read. The results of the research indicate that the information relating to various points of view and is flagged with information about the source is of the greatest importance for Internet users. The ability to critically analyze the content, the habit of checking the sources or the general orientation in the nature of contemporary mass media are key in assessing the vulnerability of societies to disinformation and manipulation on the web. In today's societies, it is the recipients of media content that the security of the entire information creation and distribution system is based on.

In the modern digital world, the web user is not able to counteract the spreading disinformation on his own, but he has an influence on the reception and classification of content in terms of assessing its authenticity. Greater awareness of the scale of the phenomenon and the ability to identify

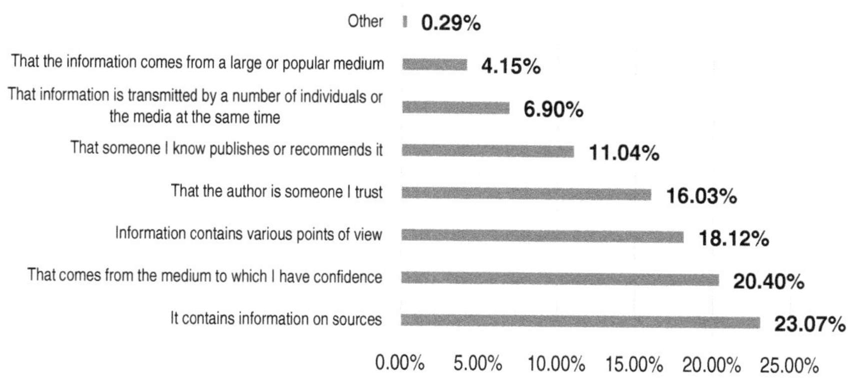

Chart 3.3 Percentage distribution of answers to the question: which of the following sources do respondents consider particularly conducive to spreading fake news?

Source: Own elaboration based on author's research.

features of disinformation reduces fears of being manipulated by the media. Expanding media competences is an expression of concern for your safety and protects against actions of people interested in misleading recipients.

The assessment of the reliability of information in cyberspace mobilizes the actions of respondents who were asked whether they check the credibility of the content, authors or profiles obtained when obtaining information from the Internet? The highest rate of 19.60% was obtained by the group of respondents who in the last three months checked the credibility of the content of damaged information on the Internet. However, the situation that results from the conducted research is disturbing, where 18.90% of the respondents do not check the credibility. On the other hand, 15.13% of respondents check the credibility of the source of information posted on the Internet. The credibility of profiles and social networking sites such as Facebook or Twitter was noted in fourth place, which accounts for 13.19% of respondents. However, the credibility of people on Facebook or Twitter is checked by only 12.01% of respondents. The results presented in the Chart 3.4 show the carelessness of the respondents as regards the lack of determination in the context of the actions taken to check the source of information, which may have an impact on social security.

Social media is the most popular source of knowledge and therefore also an environment of accumulated disinformation. Therefore, for the respondents, in the perception of manipulation and disinformation on the Internet, the source of the content and the method of its dissemination on the Internet are important. In addition, the awareness of who may be the recipient of the manipulated content gives a full picture of the threat posed by the uncritical and reckless use of content posted on the Internet.

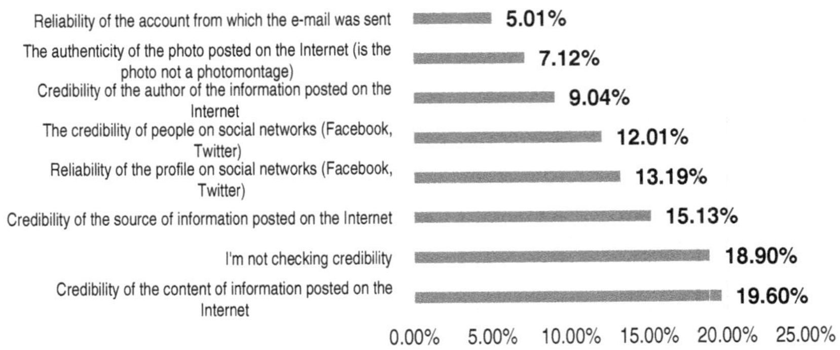

Chart 3.4 Percentage distribution of answers to the question: using the Internet in the last three months, have checked credibility in terms of?

Source: Own elaboration.

Conclusions

The development of information and communication technologies in the last dozen or so years has irretrievably changed such aspects of people's lives as work, access to information, communication, education and social relations. Developing the ability to use computer applications as well as resources and communication in the network, putting emphasis on solving problems in various fields with the conscious use of methods and tools derived from computer science, is not only an aspect facilitating the acquisition of knowledge. It is also a very important process supporting the development of many competences that are useful – if not necessary – in everyday life. Free access to the Internet creates opportunities for constant and quick retrieval of news, provides tools that are helpful in work, study, communication and entertainment. It will not be an exaggeration to say that the world has now entered an era where information has become the most valuable asset. However, while the network has become an important means of supporting the learning process, it also carries dangers such as disinformation.

The phenomenon of disinformation has been around for a long time, it is and will continue to exist. One may be tempted to say that with the development of modern societies and economies, it will occur on an increasing scale, as a result of the expanding stream of information, to which we have increasingly easier access. Manipulation in the media is also a phenomenon that we will have to deal with, whether we like it or not. The basic element of dealing with disinformation or media manipulation is broadening one's horizons with various sources of information through education.

It is important that we are aware of the consequences of disinformation and that we do not pass by it indifferently. The goal of media disinformation is to create an easily manageable society. People want to be aware that they make decisions in accordance with their own beliefs, and not caused by an artificial impulsive need caused by watching a TV program or reading information on the Internet.

It is important to be aware of possible manipulative actions and independence in the reception of media messages. Reliable knowledge acquired at school and the values learned at home should constitute the basis for effective self-defense against manipulation. In more complex "information dilemmas", support from external service providers seems to be justified.

References

Averin, A. (2018). Russia and Its Many Truths, Fake News a Roadmap. *Riga*, January, 64.

Batorowska, H., Klepka, R. and Wasiuta, O. (2019). *Media jako instrument wpływu informacyjnego i manipulacji społeczeństwem*. Kraków: LIBRON.

Consilium Europa (2020). https://www.consilium.europa.eu/pl/policies/coronavirus/fighting-disinformation.

Design102 (2019). RESIST. Counter-disinformation Toolkit.

Fallis, D. (2015). What Is Disinformation?. *Library Trends*, 63(3), 401–402.

Lawrence, A. (2020). Social Network Analysis Reveals Full Scale of Kremlin's Twitter Bot Campaign. *GlobalVoices*, 2 April 2015. https://globalvoices.org/2015/04/02/analyzing-kremlin-twitter-bots/.

McGreal, C. (2020). Vladimir Putin's "Misinformation" Offensive Prompts US to Deploy Its Cold War Propaganda Tools. *Guardian*, 25 April 2015. https://www.theguardian.com/world/2015/apr/25/us-set-to-revive-propaganda-war-as-putin-pr-machine-undermines-baltic-states.

Volchek, D. and Sindelar, D. (2020). One Professional Russian Troll Tells All. *RadioFreeEurope*, 25 March 2015. https://www.rferl.org/a/how-to-guide-russian-trolling-trolls/26919999.html.

Wasiuta, O. and Wasiuta, S. (2018). *Wojna hybrydowa Rosji przeciwko Ukrainie*. In: Klepka, R. (Ed.), *Medialne obrazy świata. Wybrane problemy społeczno-polityczne w mediach*. Kraków: Wydawnictwo Naukowe Uniwersytetu Pedagogicznego.

4 E-commerce market during the economic crisis caused by COVID-19

Małgorzata Grzelak and Paulina Owczarek

Introduction

The spread of the COVID-19 pandemic has forced the governments of almost all countries to impose severe restrictions, including limited mobility, movement and the right of assembly. A number of measures have been adopted to promote social distancing between people. Some of them resulted in the partial "freezing" of the economy as well as restrictions on the conventional forms of shopping (e.g. closing shopping malls, introducing special shopping hours for senior citizens, limiting the number of customers in shops). In addition, there has also been an increase in social anxiety caused by the fear of contamination while doing shopping or visiting public places. The above-mentioned factors led to a significant upward trend in the volume of online sales in the dynamically developing e-commerce industry.

The purpose of this chapter is to analyze the potential opportunities and threats to the e-commerce industry related to the COVID-19 pandemic, to examine the dynamics of growth in the online sales volume of products, as well as to determine the level of consumer satisfaction with online shopping and the possibility of switching to e-commerce from conventional sales channels.

Several research methods were used in the chapter. The deduction method was used to assess various observations about the restrictions related to the partial freezing of the economy and trade, while the induction method was applied in order to draw conclusions from the gathered material. Subsequently, the empirical observation method was used to diagnose the key opportunities and threats to the e-commerce industry in light of the COVID-19 pandemic, as well as to examine the dynamics of online sales volume growth and provide a short-term forecast of its development. Research material was collected from the available data and reports on the changes of e-commerce sales volumes, as well as through an analysis of survey results in the literature on the subject regarding customer satisfaction with online shopping. In addition, an analysis of a case study on the impact of the pandemic on the functioning of an e-commerce company operating in the fast-moving consumer goods (FMCG) sector, using statistical methods and the principle of statistical inference was carried out.

DOI: 10.4324/9781003285717-4

The conducted research made it possible to assess the development dynamics of the e-commerce industry in the face of the COVID-19 pandemic and to determine the changes in its sales volumes. The purpose of the questionnaire was to find answers to the following questions:

1 What percentage of the respondents actively shop online?
2 What platforms and sales channels are most often used by consumers?
3 What products are most often bought online?
4 How do the respondents assess the safety of online shopping?

The conducted research also allows to assess social moods, consumer satisfaction with online shopping and the likelihood of customers switching from conventional stationary shopping to e-commerce. In addition, it allows to draw conclusions and introduce corrective measures in order to increase the development dynamics of the e-commerce industry.

Development dynamics of the global e-commerce market in 2020

The e-commerce market is defined as the trading of goods and services through telecommunication and telecommunication tools (Babenko et al., 2019). It can also be referred to as the electronic exchange of goods using information technologies and the Internet (Chaffey, Hemphill, Edmundson-Bird, 2019). Anil Khural, in turn, defines e-commerce as the use of computer, Internet and general software to send and receive product specifications and drawings, applications, purchase orders and invoices, and any other type of data that needs to be passed on to customers, suppliers, employees or the public (How Coronavirus (COVID-19) Is Impacting Ecommerce, 2020).

In the literature on the subject, there are a number of publications dealing specifically with the impact of the COVID-19 pandemic on the e-commerce market. What is particularly worth attention are foreign publications that describe in detail the transformations taking place around the world in terms of commercial activities, business structure as well as changes in customer expectations. According to new data from Digital Commerce 360 (Anil, 2019), online retail sales in the United States increased by 30.1% year-on-year for the first six months of 2020. In June alone, a 76% growth was recorded compared to the previous year. The largest sales platform in the United States is Amazon 38.7%. Since the outbreak of the pandemic, Walmart (5.3%) and eBay (4.7%) have ranked second. The impact of COVID-19 on e-commerce varies depending on the industry. By the end of March, growth in online sales volumes was recorded for five major categories: (1) business and industrial, (2) toys and games, (3) food, beverage and tobacco, (4) office supplies and (5) health and beauty.

According to the research presented in (Bhatti et al., 2020), 52% of consumers avoid conventional shopping and crowded places. The effects of coronavirus differ depending on the nature of products, for certain products, it has been very high, while for others – less significant (Andrienko, 2020). The authors (Niazi, Shahid, Naqvi, 2020) point out that e-commerce has grown even in developing countries such as Malaysia, Singapore, Thailand and Pakistan. During the pandemic, e-commerce in Pakistan has been reported to have increased by 10% in daily record. In turn, the number of Pakistani Internet users has grown by 15%.

Retail sales of e-commerce shows that COVID-19 has significant impact on e-commerce and its sales are expected to reach $6.5 trillion by 2023. Furthermore, there are many products that are significantly impacted by the virus such as disposable gloves (670%), bread machine (652%), soups (397%), rice (386%), packaged food (377%), fruits cups (326%), milk and cream (279%), paper towel (190%) and many more (Jones, 2020).

Also, domestic literature confirms the changes that took place in Polish business after the COVID outbreak. The results of a research entitled "e-Commerce during the 2020 crisis" show (E-Commerce w czasie kryzysu, 2020) that customers often prefer online shopping. Forty-nine percent of Internet users confirmed that they had stocked up for quarantine (mostly food products, as well as cleaning agents and disinfectants). Almost half of the respondents aged 35–44 opted for online shopping. Forty-five percent of the respondents indicated that due to the threat related to the coronavirus, they decided to shop less frequently in a conventional way to reduce the risk of infection. Among the respondents who have stocked up online, 70% believed that e-commerce was currently the safest method of shopping. According to a research commissioned by Mastercard, 80% of Poles plan to continue shopping online – even after the pandemic is over.[1] In turn, the results of a research conducted by the Nilsen agency confirmed that the largest increase in online shopping was recorded in the 11th week of the year, i.e. March 9–15. The increase in sales concerned mainly such categories as cleaning agents and dry food products. From the end of February to the beginning of March, rice sales increased by 95%, flour by 84% and pasta by 65% compared to the previous year. The week when the closure of schools was announced, was the peak time when Poles were making the largest supplies, which was also reflected in the sales volumes, especially of products with a long shelf life, such as flour, pasta, groats, or water. Sales of other categories of food products also increased, including milk, eggs, meat and baby food (Portalspozywczy, 2020). The analyses presented by CRM also showed an increase in the sales of canned food, ready meals, pasta, groats, cereals and rice.[2] The president of the management board of Frisco.pl confirmed that before the pandemic, online shopping sales had been growing by 30% year-on-year, but since its outbreak, the growth rate has accelerated three to four times. An increase was recorded in the value of goods sold in March 2020 as compared to March 2019: ready meals – increase by 330% to over 630% (depending on the type of meal), canned fish – increase by 325%, fresh packaged pork – increase by 394%, fresh pates – 380%, vegetables and fruit – by 25% to 120% (Gazeta Wyborcza 2020).

However, what has been lacking in the literature on the subject is a research on the development dynamics for the industry on a national scale, accompanied with an analysis of a selected case study. Therefore, this chapter presents the characteristics of the e-commerce market development, as well as discusses examples of the impact of the pandemic on selected entities from the FMCG industry, as well as the results of a survey on changes in consumer behaviour as a result of the COVID-19 outbreak.

The unexpected outbreak of the COVID-19 pandemic forced the authorities of most countries around the world to introduce lockdowns and completely freeze the economy, which was supposed to minimize the risk of the virus spread. On the one hand, such measures resulted in shrinking of the economy, but, on the other, led to the rapid development of the e-commerce industry. The vast majority of countries around the world opted to freeze their economies in March 2020, which resulted in the growing interest of consumers in online shopping. This has been confirmed by the results of a research conducted by Google Trends on the search trends for a given term on the Internet. Charts 4.1 and 4.2 show a growing interest in the area of "online shopping" over time (comparison of 2019 and 2020) and space (indication of the most popular areas).

Chart 4.1 indicates a growing interest in the searched term in 2020. In accordance with the research methodology adopted by Google Trends, the values presented (on a scale from 0 to 100) indicate the popularity of a given term. The value of 100 indicates the highest number of searches recorded, while 50 should be interpreted as half of the number indicated above. In addition, the value of 0 means the lack of significant data allowing for conducting an analysis.

Chart 4.2 indicates a growing interest in the term "online shopping" in spatial terms. The greatest increase in the popularity of the search was recorded in Great Britain, where – during the lockdown of the economy – the term was searched for approx. five times more often than before. A threefold increase in interest was recorded in New Zealand, Ireland, Canada, Kuwait, Australia and Sri Lanka, while a twofold increase was recorded in South Africa, Belgium, the United States and Switzerland. What is interesting is that, despite the severity of the pandemic in Italy and Spain, the popularity of the search "online shopping" has not increased significantly in those countries.

The next step was an analysis of the development dynamics for the e-commerce market in light of the COVID-19 pandemic. Table 4.1 shows the fluctuation in the value of the global e-commerce market in 2017–2020 and the

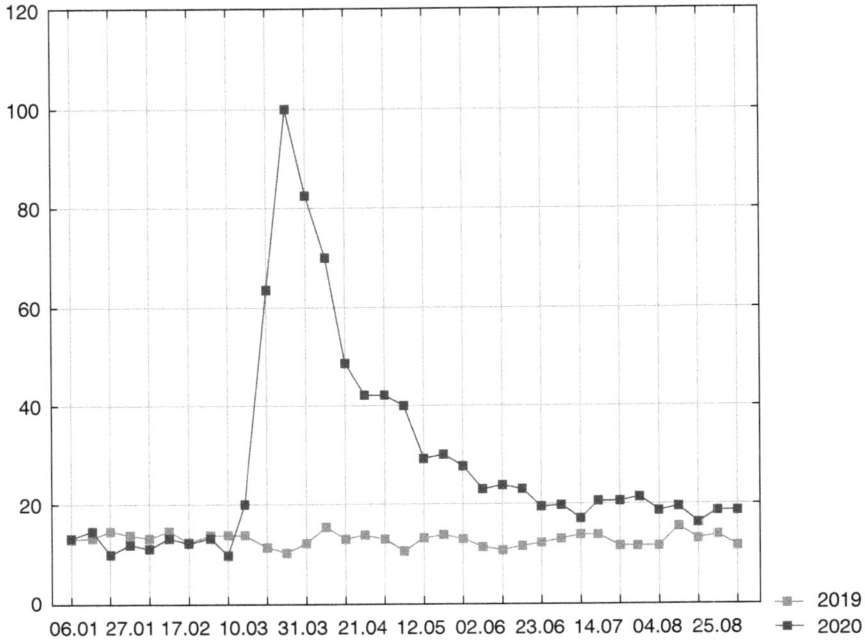

Chart 4.1 Search trends for the "online shopping" term in 2019 and 2020.
Source: Own elaboration based on a research conducted by Google Trends.

forecast for its development until 2023. It should be noted that the annual increase in the market size is estimated at approximately 20%. In addition, the share of this sector in the total market is expected to increase. The continuing pandemic and its subsequent outbreaks will drive the development of the e-commerce market and generate permanent changes in consumer shopping behaviour.

The outbreak of the pandemic forced the need to update forecasts for the development of both the retail trade and its electronic sector. Earlier estimates (an increase for retail trade by 4.4% to the level of USD 26,460 trillion and for e-commerce by 18.4% to the level of USD 4.106 trillion) were lowered by 10% for retail trade and by 2% for e-commerce (https://www.emarketer.com/content/global-ecommerce-2019, 2020). Nonetheless, experts agree that the countries that are likely to experience the greatest development of the e-commerce market include the Philippines, Malaysia and Spain – namely countries that were severely affected by the first wave of COVID-19 (Oberlo, 2020). In 2020, Asian and Pacific countries have had the largest share in the global e-commerce market, among which China has played the key role (63% of the global market value). The countries of North America

Chart 4.2 Search popularity for the "online shopping" term in regions.
Source: Own elaboration based on a research conducted by Google Trends.

Table 4.1 Value of the global e-commerce market in 2017–2023

Year	*Value (USD trillion)*	*Increase in market size (%)*	*E-commerce market share in total retail market (%)*
2017	2382	28	10.4
2018	2982	22.9	12.2
2019	3535	20.7	14.1
2020	4206	19	16.1
2021	4927	18.1	17.1
2022	5695	20	15.6
2023	6542	22	14.9

Source: Own elaboration based on: https://www.emarketer.com/content/global-ecommerce-2019, 2020.

(19%) and Western Europe (13%) have ranked second (13%) (Chart 4.3) (Emarketer, 2020).

The countries with the largest global e-commerce markets (listed in the order of decreasing value in trillion USD) include the United States, China, Great Britain, Japan, Germany, France and Canada. A detailed analysis of the size of e-commerce markets in selected countries and regions is presented in Tables 4.2–4–7.

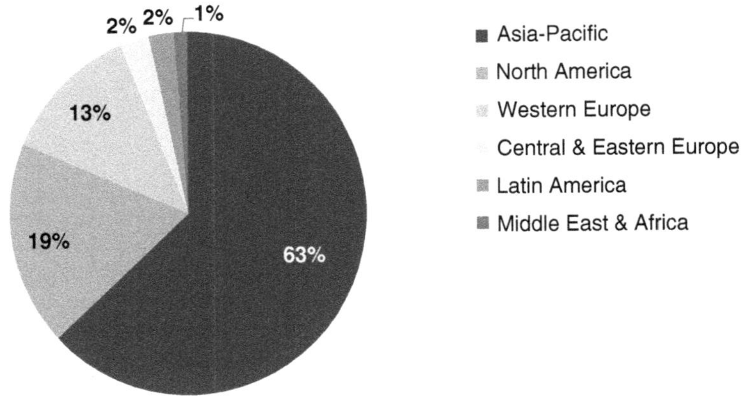

Chart 4.3 Retail e-commerce sales worldwide by region, 2020.

Source: Own elaboration based on: https://www.emarketer.com/content/global-ecommerce-2019, 2020.

Table 4.2 Value of the e-commerce market in the USA in 2018–2022

Year	*Trillion USD*	*Percentage of total retail sales*
2018	523.64	13.6
2019	601.65	11.0
2020	709.78	14.5
2021	765.17	14.4
2022	859.28	15.5

Source: Own elaboration based on: https://www.emarketer.com/content/global-ecommerce-2019, 2020.

Table 4.3 Value of the e-commerce market in China in 2018–2024

Year	*Trillion USD*	*Percentage of total retail sales*
2018	489.6	13.6
2019	528.3	11.0
2020	507.2	14.5
2021	533.0	14.4
2022	554.9	15.5
2023	582.6	15.6
2024	612.3	15.4

Source: Own elaboration based on: https://www.emarketer.com/content/global-ecommerce-2019, 2020.

In each of the presented cases, an upward trend in the development of the value of the e-commerce market is noticeable. In addition, along with the size of this segment, its share in total retail sales in a given country increases. The outbreak of the coronavirus pandemic, far from stopping this trend, has accelerated the pace of development of online sales.

Table 4.4 Value of the e-commerce market in Germany in 2019–2023

Year	*Trillion USD*	*Percentage of total retail sales*
2019	79.47	8.9
2020	92.33	11.2
2021	96.94	10.9
2022	103.24	11.2
2023	108.10	11.5

Source: Own elaboration based on: https://www.emarketer.com/content/global-ecommerce-2019, 2020.

Table 4.5 Value of the e-commerce market in Canada in 2019–2024

Year	*Trillion USD*	*Percentage of total retail sales*
2019	43.11	6.8
2020	52.04	8.7
2021	58.54	9.4
2022	65.27	10.1
2023	72.45	10.9
2024	79.84	10.2

Source: Own elaboration based on: https://www.emarketer.com/content/global-ecommerce-2019, 2020.

Table 4.6 Value of the e-commerce market in France in 2019–2023

Year	*Trillion USD*	*Percentage of total retail sales*
2019	66.00	9.2
2020	77.27	12.2
2021	83.76	11.9
2022	90.38	12.4
2023	96.43	13.0

Source: Own elaboration based on: https://www.emarketer.com/content/global-ecommerce-2019, 2020.

Table 4.7 Value of the e-commerce market in Latin America in 2018–2023

Year	*Trillion USD*	*Percentage of total retail sales*
2018	56.47	3.5
2019	70.07	4.4
2020	83.63	5.6
2021	94.73	6.2
2022	105.42	6.6
2023	116.23	7.7

Source: Own elaboration based on: https://www.emarketer.com/content/global-ecommerce-2019, 2020.

Case study of the consequences of COVID-19 on online sales in the FMCG industry

The analysis covers the impact of the COVID-19 pandemic on the sales of FMCG products via one of the Polish online sales platforms. The business activity of the entity subject to the research consists in providing its customers with the highest quality certified organic food from Poland and other countries on all continents. It is the leader of the Polish market in the production and distribution of organic food, with over 6,000 food products, including fresh products such as dairy, vegetables, fruit and meat products.

The main area of the research was the impact of the COVID-19 pandemic on the number of orders placed online and the increase in demand for transportation services used to deliver orders to customers. The research sample consisted of DAF, SCANIA and MAN vehicles with a maximum permissible weight of 40 tons and a load weight of up to 19 tons. A total of 1,332 observations regarding orders placed in the period between January 1, 2019 and July 31, 2020 were analyzed. The dependent variables were the average daily mileage of the vehicle and the weight of the transported load, as well as the revenue obtained by the company in each month.

The first step was an analysis of the variability of the size of the tested parameters (i.e. average vehicle mileage, load weight and generated revenue) for each month (Table 4.8).

The subsequent step was a detailed variability analysis of the parameters in question in individual groups. First, the compliance of individual variables with the normal distribution was verified. For this purpose, the Kolmogorov–Smirnov test was used. Its null hypothesis assumes that the distribution of the examined feature in the population is its normal distribution. Considering the obtained results, the null hypothesis had to be rejected in favour of the alternative hypothesis, thus confirming that the distribution of the examined variables was not consistent with normal distribution (Table 4.9).

In the next step, an analysis of the dependent variables divided according to the vehicle brand was carried out in terms of the possibility of their aggregation for further analysis. As the distribution of the examined variables was not normal, the non-parametric Kruskal–Wallis test was used, which compared each observation in terms of the median. The null hypothesis of the above-mentioned test was that all samples came from the same population, i.e. that there were no statistically significant differences between them. The results of the test are presented in Table 4.10. For the daily mileage variable, the calculated p value is 0.14, which means that the null hypothesis should be assumed for the adopted significance level $\alpha = 0.05$, and therefore, there are no significant differences between the variability of the median value depending on the vehicle brand (Chart 4.4). Hence, a further analysis of this variable was performed jointly for all vehicles.

Table 4.8 Variability of the average value of the daily mileage, load weight and revenue depending on the vehicle model

Year	*Month*	*Brand*								
		DAF			*MAN*			*SCANIA*		
		Daily mileage (km)	*Load weight (kg)*	*Revenue (PLN)*	*Daily mileage (km)*	*Load weight (kg)*	*Revenue (PLN)*	*Daily mileage (km)*	*Load weight (kg)*	*Revenue (PLN)*
2019	1	374	18556	913	417	18222	759	398	17630	980
2019	2	380	18669	842	358	17809	699	376	17579	945
2019	3	338	18461	816	330	17977	690	315	17853	734
2019	4	265	18677	806	274	18050	611	284	17553	732
2019	5	354	18405	770	378	18096	760	345	17184	722
2019	6	344	18575	839	350	18080	680	351	17665	843
2019	7	334	18639	851	327	18077	614	388	17760	775
2019	8	367	18567	820	370	18310	620	392	17985	807
2019	9	381	18750	979	362	18118	697	386	17341	777
2019	10	391	18643	920	420	18000	702	425	17495	808
2019	11	423	18386	1100	364	18159	548	304	17518	734
2019	12	338	18674	697	293	18000	530	305	17794	698
2020	1	373	19000	753	425	18000	861	431	17965	650
2020	2	377	19000	928	358	18000	775	381	17971	809
2020	3	372	19000	746	423	18037	996	492	18440	1214
2020	4	402	19040	1050	378	18123	953	429	18308	1094
2020	5	443	19000	1082	404	18000	987	429	18077	1107
2020	6	368	19000	947	356	18000	796	309	18000	733
2020	7	310	19000	817	312	18000	792	308	18000	640

Source: Own elaboration.

Table 4.9 Results of the Kolmogorov–Smirnov test for the examined variables

Variable	*DAF*		*SCANIA*		*MAN*	
	K–S test		*K–S test*		*K–S test*	
	Value of the test statistic	*p*	*Value of the test statistic*	*p*	*Value of the test statistic*	*p*
Mileage	0.09	0.00	0.11	0.00	0.10	0.00
Load weight	0.47	0.00	0.36	0.00	0.47	0.00
Revenue	0.13	0.00	0.16	0.00	0.13	0.00

Source: Own elaboration.

Table 4.10 The results of the Kruskal–Wallis test for individual variables

Variable	*The value of the K–W test statistic*	*p-Value*
Daily mileage	3.96	0.14
Load weight	449.46	0.00
Revenue	64.87	0.00

Source: Own elaboration.

On the other hand, in the K–W test for the variables "load weight" and "vehicle mileage", the obtained p value was 0.00, which means that the null hypothesis should be rejected in favour of the alternative hypothesis. It means there are significant differences in the above-mentioned parameters depending on the vehicle brand; therefore, further analysis was carried out taking into account this variable (Charts 4.5 and 4.6).

Then, the dynamics of the examined variables for individual months covered by the research was compared. In the first step, the variability of the vehicle mileage was analyzed. The test was carried out for all vehicles in total (Chart 4.7).

The Kruskal–Wallis test was also carried out for the above-mentioned variable, for which the obtained value was $p = 0.00$, which means differences between the median mileage values for individual months were significant. On this basis, multiple comparisons of mean ranks were conducted for all tests, the results of which indicate significant differences between the mileage values for individual months. However, this variability results from factors other than the outbreak of the COVID-19 pandemic. It can be concluded that despite the outbreak of the pandemic, the network of recipients and product distribution within the examined entity did not change significantly.

In the subsequent step, the load weight variable was analyzed. The analysis was carried out for individual groups according to the vehicle brand. Due to the lack of normal distribution of the examined variables, the Kruskal–Wallis test was repeated, in order to show whether there were significant differences between the volume of the transported cargo before and during the pandemic. The test results are presented in Table 4.11.

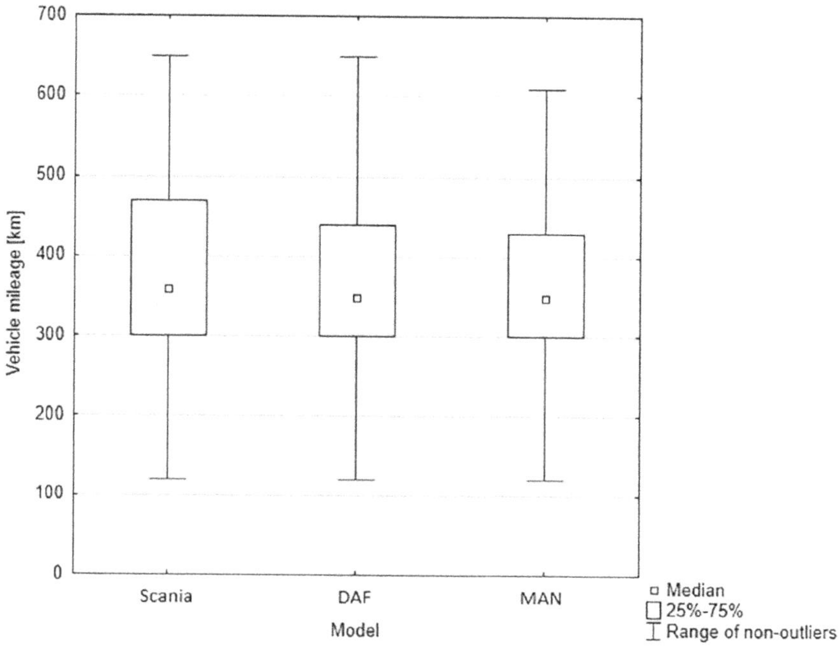

Chart 4.4 Box plot of the monthly mileage median depending on the vehicle brand.
Source: Own elaboration.

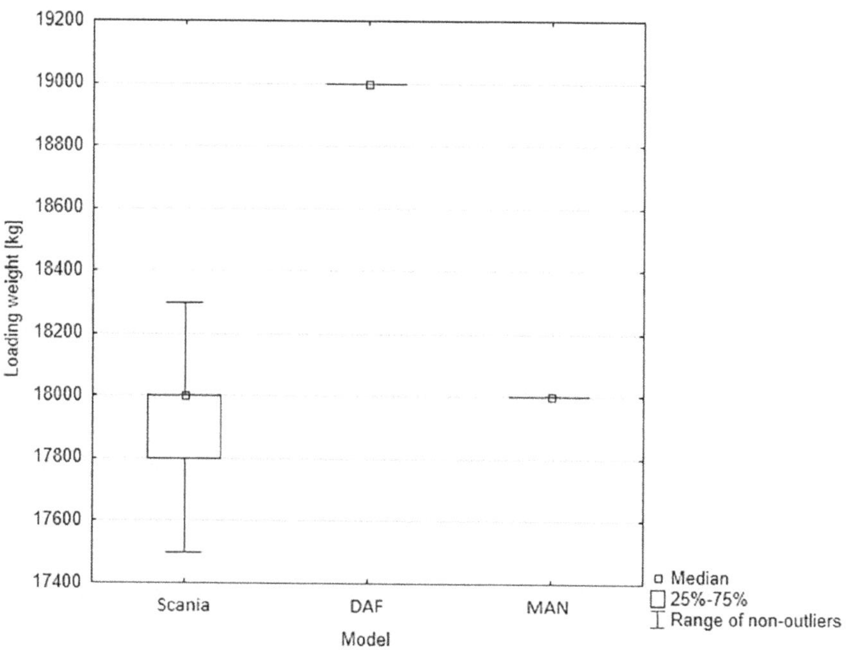

Chart 4.5 Box plot of the load weight median depending on the vehicle brand.
Source: Own elaboration.

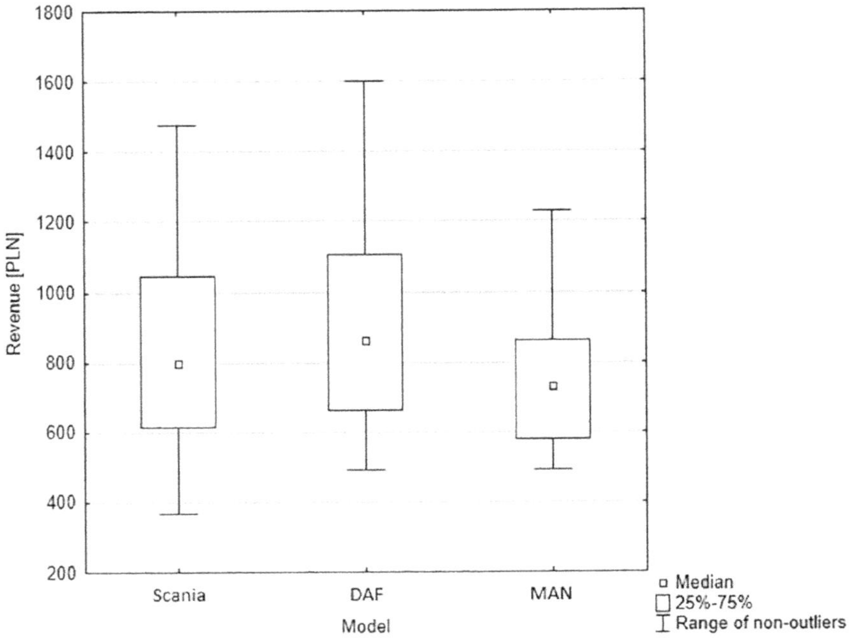

Chart 4.6 Box plot of the revenue median depending on the vehicle brand.
Source: Own elaboration.

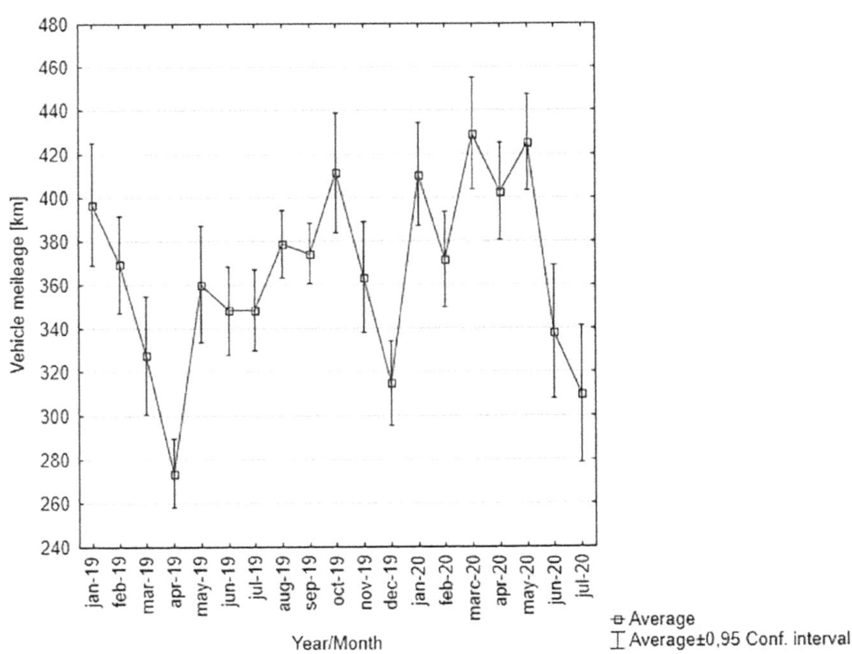

Chart 4.7 Average monthly mileage of vehicles in the company in individual months.
Source: Own elaboration.

The results of the test show that there were no significant differences in the weight of the transported load for MAN vehicles. The calculated p value was 0.14; therefore, the null hypothesis was confirmed. This is shown in the chart of the average monthly load weight over the time period covered by the research (Chart 4.8). This means that the COVID-19 pandemic did not have a significant impact on the volume of the transported load for this vehicle.

The situation was opposite for SCANIA and DAF vehicles. For the conducted K–W test, the p value was 0.00, which means that for these vehicles, the differences in the weight of the transported cargo for individual months were statistically significant. In the following step, multiple comparisons were conducted for mean ranks of all samples of the above-mentioned vehicles. On this basis, it can be concluded that within the examined period, there was a significant increase in the weight of the delivered cargo, especially in

Table 4.11 The results of the Kruskal–Wallis test for the significance of differences in the median load mass for individual months

Variable load weight	*The value of the K–W test statistic*	*p-Value*
MAN	3.96	0.14
DAF	449.46	0.00
SCANIA	64.87	0.00

Source: Own elaboration.

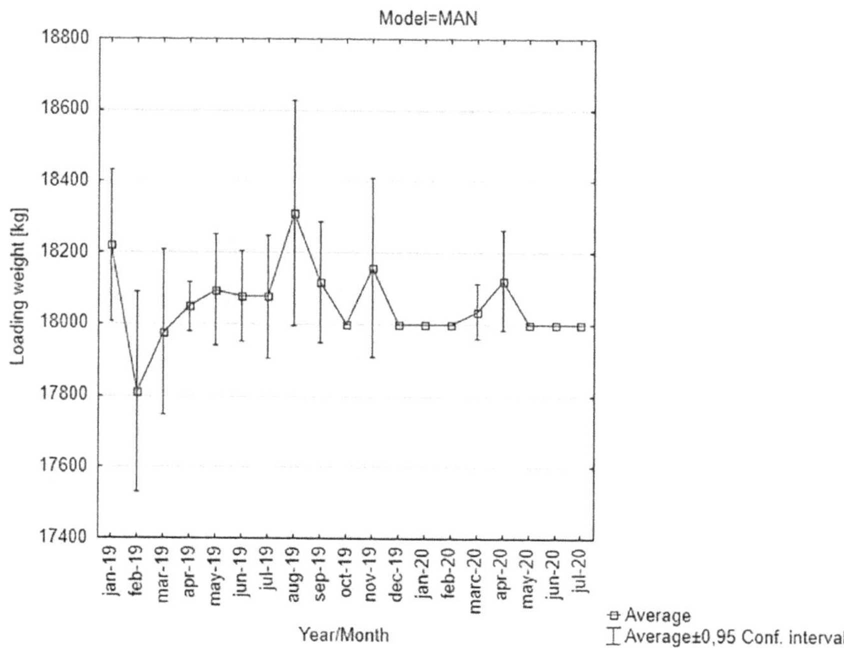

Chart 4.8 Average monthly load weight of cargo transported by MAN vehicles in individual months.

Source: Own elaboration.

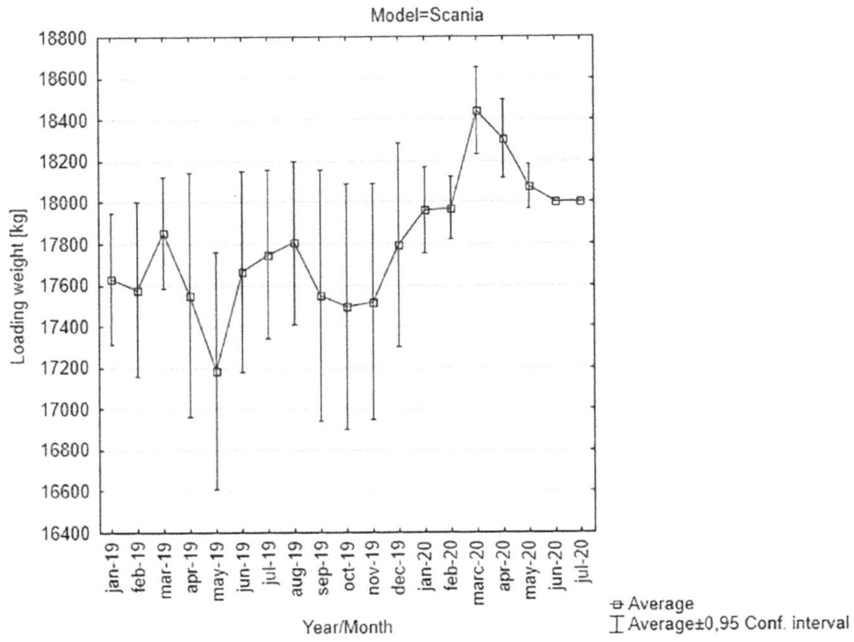

Chart 4.9 Average monthly weight of cargo transported by SCANIA vehicles in individual months.

Source: Own elaboration.

March and April, when a full lockdown was imposed in Poland (Charts 4.9 and 4.10). It means that the coronavirus pandemic had a significant impact on the purchasing behaviour of consumers, encouraging them to switch to e-commerce or m-commerce (mobile commerce).

The third examined variable was the company's monthly revenue generated depending on the vehicle brand. Again, due to the lack of normal distribution of the examined variable, the Kruskal–Wallis test was used to check whether there were significant differences in the time period in question (Table 4.12).

The conducted K–W test showed statistically significant differences in the monthly revenue generated depending on the vehicle brand. In addition, multiple comparisons of mean ranks for all samples showed that in the case of MAN and SCANIA brands, a significant increase in revenue from sales and distribution of goods was recorded in March, April and May 2020, which proves a significant impact of the COVID-19 pandemic on financial results.

The situation was quite the opposite for the DAF brand. The results of the K–W test indicate significant differences in revenue for the time period in question. However, further detailed analysis did not show any correlation

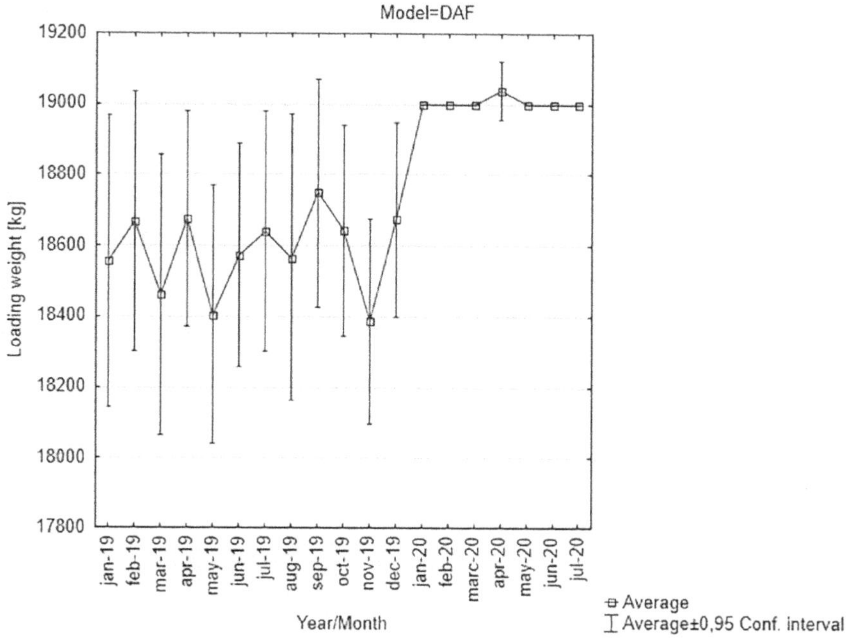

Chart 4.10 Average monthly weight of cargo transported by DAF vehicles in individual months.

Source: Own elaboration.

Table 4.12 The results of the Kruskal–Wallis test for the significance of differences in the median revenue for individual months

Monthly revenue variable	*The value of the K–W test statistic*	*p-Value*
MAN	166.00	0.00
DAF	97.46	0.00
SCANIA	156.53	0.00

Source: Own elaboration.

between the above-mentioned trend and the outbreak of the pandemic. The Mann–Whitney U test was conducted to compare the revenue in April 2019 and 2020, for which the null hypothesis was that the samples came from one population. The obtained p value was 0.00, which means that the revenue increased year on year. Nevertheless, the obtained revenue for this brand during the pandemic was at the same level that had been recorded immediately before the outbreak, and therefore, its impact on this variable cannot be considered significant.

The last step was an analysis of the variable "monthly revenue" for the entire company. The above-mentioned variable is the most significant, as it

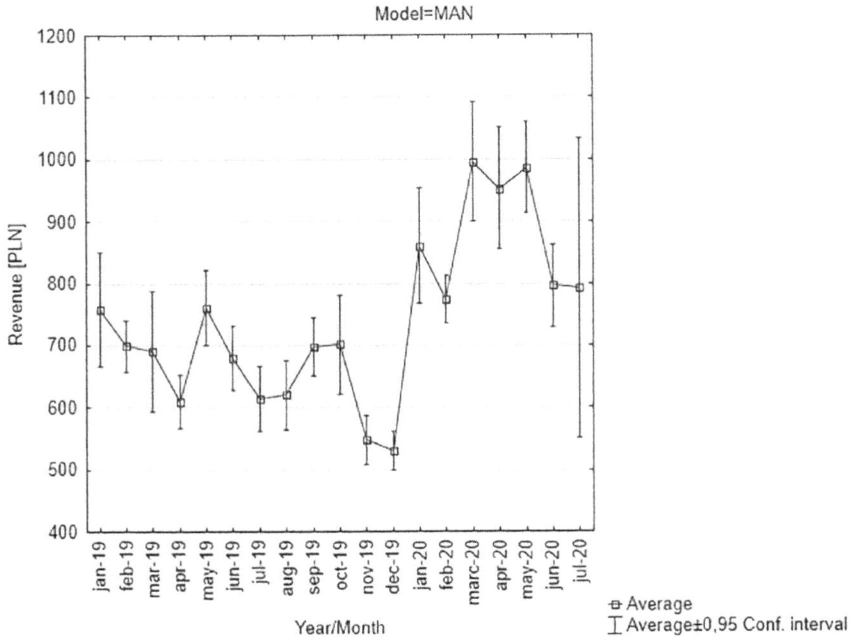

Chart 4.11 Average monthly revenue of the company in individual months.
Source: Own elaboration.

may indicate the fluctuations in the value of the e-commerce market during the pandemic. Chart 4.11 shows the average revenue of the company during the examined period.

It should be noted that a significant increase in revenue was recorded after the restrictions and the lockdown were imposed in Poland. What is also important is the fact that with the temporary unfreezing of the economy, the company's revenue dropped to the level from before the first wave of the pandemic. This is why the management should conduct a detailed analysis of the situation, as well as introduce improvements, which could allow to secure higher revenue in the event of a second and subsequent waves of the virus.

Survey of consumer behaviour in the post-COVID reality

In the subsequent part of the research, an analysis of survey results from the available literature on the subject was performed. At first, the percentage share of respondents declaring to actively use online shopping was verified and the impact of the COVID-19 pandemic on this factor was determined. The research was conducted on a group of 2001 respondents with a diversified age structure (Omni-commerce, 2020) who were asked whether they actively used online shopping. The answers are shown in Chart 4.12.

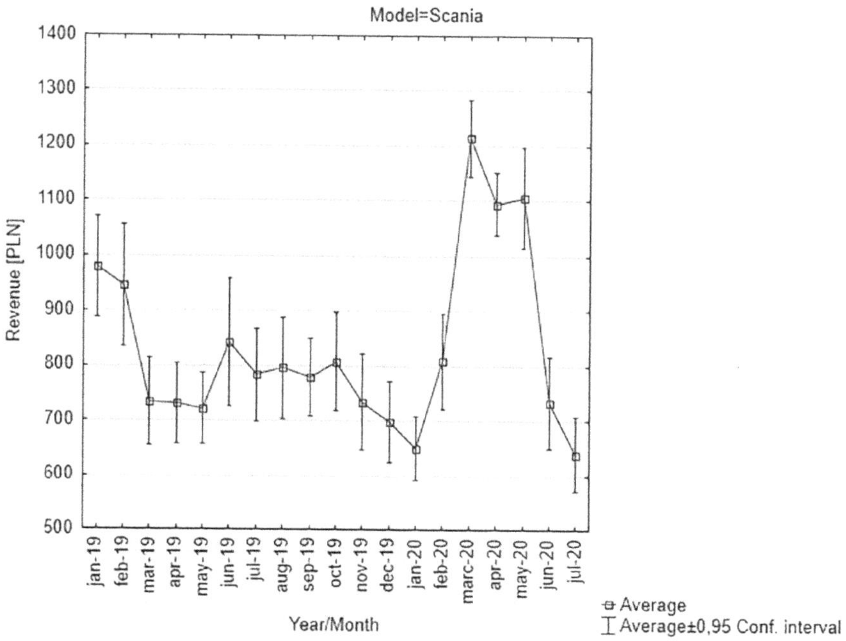

Chart 4.12 Answers to the question: do you actively use online shopping?
Source: Own elaboration based on: Omni-commerce (2020); E-Commerce w czasie kryzysu (2020).

The vast majority of the respondents declared to actively use online sales channel. In addition, it has been an upward trend year by year. A particularly high increase in the growth rate was recorded following the COVID-19 outbreak.

Then, an analysis was conducted in terms of the platforms and sales channels most frequently used by consumers. The most popular channels for concluding remote transactions were online shops (52% of respondents in 2020). Purchasing and auction platforms (38%) and price comparison websites (16%) ranked second and third, respectively – Chart 4.13.

In addition, an analysis was also conducted in terms of the most frequently purchased categories of products (Chart 4.14).

Electronic articles were among the most frequently purchased items in 2020. This can be explained mainly by the switch to remote work and learning, and the need to ensure adequate equipment for home offices. An increase in online sales volumes was also observed for food products and pharmaceuticals. In turn, a drop in customer interest was recorded for products from such categories as baby goods, home and garden and tourism.

The last step was to evaluate the perceived safety of online shopping (E-Commerce w czasie kryzysu, 2020). The respondents were asked whether,

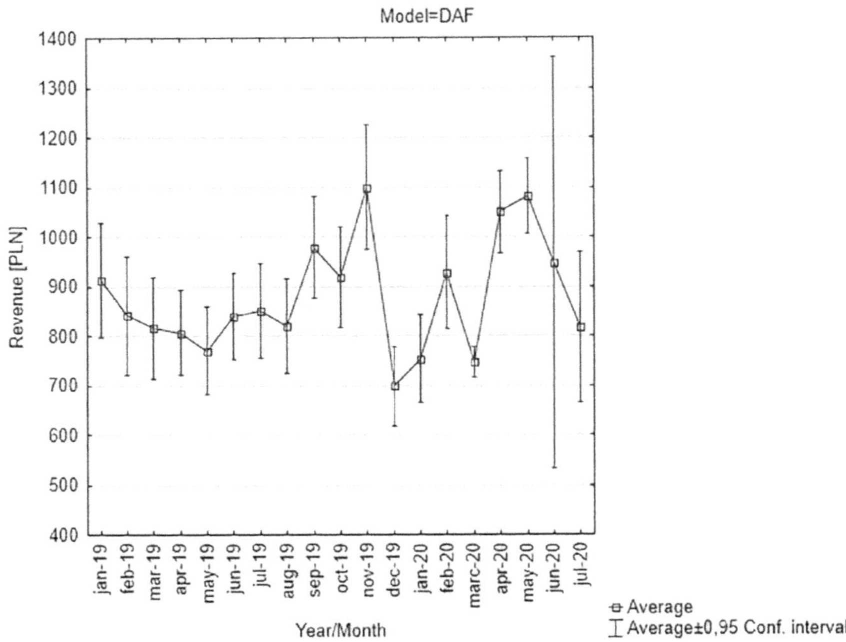

Chart 4.13 Answers to the question about the sales platforms and channels most often used by consumers.

Source: Own elaboration based on: Omni-commerce (2020); E-Commerce w czasie kryzysu (2020).

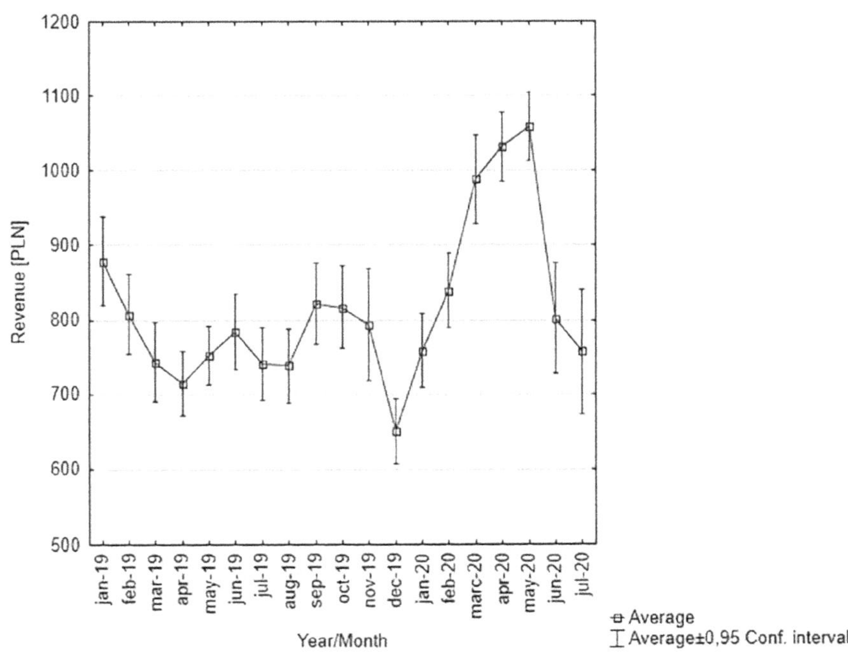

Chart 4.14 Categories of products most frequently purchased online.

Source: Own elaboration based on: Omni-commerce (2020); E-Commerce w czasie kryzysu (2020).

in their opinion, online shopping was safer during the pandemic than visiting stationary shops. Out of 1,200 respondents, 47% indicated online channels as definitely safer than shopping in stationary shops, 24% – as rather safer, 22% – as rather not safer, while 7% declared them as definitely not safer. This indicates that the COVID-19 pandemic has had a significant impact on the development of the e-commerce market.

Conclusions

To conclude, the purpose of this chapter was to analyze the potential opportunities and threats related to the e-commerce industry in light of the outbreak of the COVID-19 pandemic, to examine the growth dynamics of online sales volumes of products, as well as to determine the level of consumer satisfaction with online shopping and the possibility of switching to e-commerce from conventional sales channels. In order to do that, the development trends of the e-commerce market, both at the global level and at the level of selected countries, including the USA, China, France and Germany, were analyzed. The analysis indicated that the outbreak of the pandemic had had a positive impact on the development of the analyzed segment, especially in countries heavily affected by the first wave of the virus.

The second part of the chapter was a case study of a company from the FMCG sector and the impact of the COVID-19 pandemic on its functioning. The study showed that the structure of the distribution network of goods to customers did not change due to the pandemic, and the average monthly mileage of vehicles remained at the same level. What changed was the weight of the transported cargo, as a result of which the company's revenue increased, mainly during the period of the full lockdown in Poland (i.e. in March, April and May 2020). The analysis showed that the revenue decreased after the first outbreak, when the lockdown was lifted. For this reason, the company management should pay special attention to the factors that had an impact on the mentioned fluctuations. The managers should also implement corrective actions in order to prevent the decline in revenue and enable further development of online sales, especially during the upcoming second wave of infections.

The third step was an analysis of surveys in the available literature on the subject regarding consumer purchasing trends during the COVID-19 pandemic. It was found that the vast majority of customers had switched to online shopping, and approx. 72% of the respondents declared they were actively using online shopping. In addition, online shops were indicated as the most frequently chosen platforms for concluding remote transactions (52% of respondents in 2020), followed by purchasing and auction platforms (38%) and price comparison websites (16%). In turn, an analysis of the categories of products indicated that the most frequently purchased items in 2020 were electronic products, which was mainly due to the need to switch to remote work and learning, and the need to ensure adequate equipment for home offices. An increase in consumers' interest was also observed for food products and pharmaceuticals, while a drop was recorded for such categories as baby goods, home and garden and tourism categories.

The above-mentioned observations allowed for a comprehensive analysis of the development dynamics of the global and local e-commerce markets in light of the outbreak of the COVID-19 pandemic, as well as trends in consumer behaviour as a result of the situation. In addition, the presented case study, with a comprehensive analysis of the basic parameters of the functioning of entities and their financial results, can be used by entrepreneurs (mainly from the segment of small, micro and medium-sized enterprises) to develop a plan of corrective and remedial measures leading to the improvement of the presented indicators and variables, despite the lack of professional structures for data analysis.

Notes

1 A survey conducted by an independent research institute Fly Research, on a sample of 10,000 adults surveyed from 16 European countries in June 2020.
2 CMR data – Market Monitoring Center – Panel of Small Format Shops up to 300 m^2 and Supermarkets from 301 to 2,500 m^2, Period: 24.02.–01.03.2020.

References

Andrienko, O. (2020). *Ecommerce & Consumer Trends during Coronavirus*. https://www.semrush.com/blog/ecommerce-covid-19/.

Anil, K. (2019). *Introduction to E-Commerce*. http://www.ddegjust.ac.in/studymaterial/mcom/mc201.pdf.

Babenko, V. et al. (2019). Factors of the Development of International E-Commerce under the Conditions of Globalization. *SHS Web of Conferences*, 65, 04016.

Bhatti, A. et al. (2020) E-Commerce Trends during COVID-19 Pandemic. *International Journal of Future Generation Communication and Networking*, 13(2), 1449–1452.

Chaffey, D., Hemphill, T. and Edmundson-Bird, D. (2019). *Digital Business and E-commerce Management*. London, UK: Pearson.

E-Commerce w czasie kryzysu (2020). Izba Gospodarki Elektronicznej. Mobile Institute.

Emarketer (2020). https://www.emarketer.com/content/global-ecommerce-2019.

Gazeta Wyborcza (2020). https://wyborcza.pl/7,156282,25799648,prezes-frisco-pl-w-szczycie-paniki-w-jednym-dniu-sprzedalismy.html#s=BoxOpImg3.

How Coronavirus (COVID-19) Is Impacting Ecommerce. (2020). https://www.roi-revolution.com/blog/2020/08/coronavirus-and-ecommerce/.

Jones, K. (2020). *COVID-19 the Pandemic Economy: What Are Shoppers Buying Online during COVID-19*. https: https://www.visualcapitalist.com/shoppers-buying-online-ecommerce-covid-19/.

Niazi, A., Shahid, A. and Naqvi, H. (2020). *The Pandemic Is E-commerce's Time to Shine. But Will It Last?*. https://profit.pakistantoday.com.pk/2020/05/04/the-pandemic-is-e-commerces-time-to-shine-but-will-it-last/.

Oberlo (2020). https://www.oberlo.com/statistics/ecommerce-sales-by-country.

Omni-commerce: kupuję wygodnie (2020). Izba Gospodarki Elektronicznej.

Portalspozywczy (2020). https://www.portalspozywczy.pl/handel/wiadomosci/nielsen-polacy-zaczeli-robic-zakupy-na-zapas, 181932.html.

5 Customer evolution in terms of digital development and purchasing decisions during a pandemic security and risk

Wioletta Wereda, Jacek Woźniak and Wojciech Włodarkiewicz

Introduction

In the modern world, we have experienced two major changes since the second decade of the 21st century. Firstly, a new, digital socialism (or digital activism, i.e. a social movement in which citizens, using ICT tools, show the need to influence social, economic and political reality) emerged in the market, in which the masses equipped with the means of production self-organize, creating such so-called "hyperarchic structures", they work for free towards a common goal and then share and use the "fruits" of cooperation free of charge. Secondly, one of the worst crises – the coronavirus pandemic – which is just beginning to "crumble" and the world starts to rebuild socially and economically. As COVID-19 took its economic and emotional toll on the world, businesses and customers were – and still are – faced with myriad uncertainties.

With reference to cyberactivism, the following levels of cooperation can be distinguished, while it should be noted that in each of them the level of complexity of consumer cooperation increases (Kelly, 1995, pp. 22–23; Roszkowska-Menkes, 2015, pp. 99–100; Shirky, 2010, pp. 130–135; Wereda, Moch, 2000):

1 Level one (sharing) – through such websites as YouTube, Facebook (FB), Instagram and other online forums, Internet users share practically everything, from information about themselves, their well-being, their location, through photos, videos, music, to interesting news, articles, opinions on products and services; it is the simplest and least demanding form of networking that forms the foundation for the next, more advanced levels of engagement.
2 Level two (conversation) – commenting on blog entries, YouTube videos or friends' activities on FB is the first step necessary to move to the next level, i.e. to start group cooperation. Groups whose main activity is mere exchange are simply a collection of individuals, but when these individuals begin to communicate with each other and then collaborate, a group identity is produced.

DOI: 10.4324/9781003285717-5

3 Level three (cooperation) – takes place when units work together to achieve a common goal; at this level, cooperation requires, to some extent, negotiation and group decisions; an example of cooperation may be the so-called cyber-activists undertaken in order to work out social changes or influence specific institutions; at this level, partner production is also undertaken, defined as "a method of producing goods and services, based entirely on self-organizing egalitarian communities of people who voluntarily form a group striving to achieve a common goal". The final product is the result of the work of each of the project participants and would not be possible without their input, e.g. Wikipedia.
4 Level four (collective action) – the most difficult, the most advanced and at the same time the rarest level of group initiatives in the network; project participants commit to making a joint effort towards a specific goal, assume joint responsibility for the project and group decisions are binding on all; group cohesion becomes a critical factor in achieving the desired result.

The year 2020 around the world meant that not only each of us experiences the new reality and tries to adapt to it efficiently, but we also analyze and try to predict its short- and long-term effects. The phenomena we are currently struggling with are unique in that they affect everyone on many levels. What is more, the mutual dependencies and connections, which previously societies often did not realize or did not appreciate, are very clearly visible. Each person is currently subjected to a number of challenges, both as an individual – consumer, employee, entrepreneur, citizen, but also activities within entire organizations or society (PWC Report, 2020). Before our eyes and with our participation, new consumer behaviours and habits are formed, especially after taking into account the risks that appear in everyday reality and cyber space. In connection with the above, each client must take care of his safety, because forced to lockdown, he becomes less vigilant and is obliged to spend more time in the network. The purpose of this chapter is to present the customer's evolution in digital development and purchasing decisions during a pandemic, with a focus on safety and risk.

The digital age and the evolution of the customer on the market

The beginning of the 21st century is a period of further acceleration of the pace of scientific discoveries, leading to profound socio-economic changes. The level of global expenditure on research and development is growing year by year and until the pandemic period after 2010, an increasing number of patent applications were registered worldwide, and in 2018, patent applications filed worldwide reached 3.3 million (Report "World Intellectual Property Indicators 2019", 2019, p. 12). On the one hand, further radical technologies are the fruit of intensive research. On the other hand, scientists are constantly looking for new applications for existing technologies. The progressive convergence of technology is also a characteristic phenomenon of the modern world of science and business. The result of these processes is the constant appearance of these complex products and services, more and more often combining solutions from many different industries. The dynamically developing fields include, among others, astronautics, electronics, bio- and nanotechnology. However, it can be noticed that the greatest impact on society and economy seems to have information and communication technologies, which during the pandemic permeate almost all forms of human activity (Roszkowska-Menkes, 2015, p. 81). Therefore, digital transformation has been with us for years, but it is still one of the biggest challenges facing organizations. The current situation shows that it is not just a choice, but more of a business ultimatum – to be or not to be. As a result of the COVID-19 pandemic, it has evolved to be a key element that provides the possibility of survival, because it not only enables the continuity of operation of most organizations, but also allows them to develop and build their confidence in changing times. It affects all aspects of the enterprise, it is a complex and continuous process, requiring learning, using new technologies and dealing with previously unknown challenges. In all this, we should remember about customers and employees who are the most important in the entire digitization process (Report "13 faktów o cyfryzacji", 2020, p. 4). Moreover, many scientists and practitioners note that digital transformation, which is a change in the way an organization operates through the use of digital technologies and data, as well as a change in people's mentality, is always a process and an evolution. In fact, every business is people who have been working for it for years, technologies that have already been invested in, products and services currently offered to consumers, knowledge, processes, structures and many other elements – and all of these must be taken into account, changed, optimized or used in a new way. Customer needs do not undergo revolutionary changes, rather the ways of satisfying these needs are changing. For example, people still want to watch series and movies, but not necessarily in the cinema or on traditional TV, hence the arrival of Netflix and other VOD (Video on Demand) platforms. Transformations do not break out suddenly, but are rather the result of many years of cumulative changes. Netflix itself began by sending DVDs by post with fees in the subscription model, which allowed to avoid penalties for detention, which was a significant change in the model of providing services to the then current market rental companies.

It should be remembered that it is the digital era, also called the fourth era, that is the era of digitization and the network, the main feature of which is unlimited connectivity and global reach. Thanks to this network, more than 7 billion people around the world stay in touch. They also exchange information, knowledge and online purchases with each other using this network. The process also involves billions of electronic devices and machines with artificial intelligence installed and used by humans (Skinner, 2018, p. 31).

The digital age is also presented in literature as the reconstruction era. This term reflects the activities of this era on every sphere of the organization's activity – the re-profiling of the entire business environment of enterprises, the manner of customer service and the product range released to the market. It focuses its resources primarily on the use of modern solutions and combining them with appropriate means of mass communication in order to translocate huge databases. The reconstruction era is defined as the stage in which the business models of enterprises, their methods of operation, were dictated by changes taking place in digitization (Adamczewski, 2018, pp. 14–15). The year 1990, considered the birth of the Internet, led to the transition to a new generation of information and technology every 10 years. Contemporary authors believe that humanity is slowly entering the next decade called Web 4.0 (Skinner, 2016, p. 41).

Figure 5.1 shows the evolution of the Internet from Web 1.0 to Web 4.0. The first stage of evolution created the network that appeared first and was used mainly by enterprises that wanted to promote themselves on the Internet. The content posted was static content, that is, content that was delivered to users in the same version or that contained the content of databases from a set that were published to recipients. The pages consisted of little extensive content, while the web browsers were "modestly" extensive (Narayana, Colarelli O'Connor, 2010, p. 505). The first website was designed in 1991 by Tim Berbers-Lee. The vast majority of websites were created by universities and research institutes to present to the public a list of the collected knowledge. Another feature of this generation was control over the pages and organizing the content (Skinner, 2018, pp. 41–43).

The advent of Web 2.0 brought about the start of online sales, as well as the development of payment services. In this decade, Internet publishing platforms also began to emerge, offering the construction of websites and blogs. Web 2.0 is also associated with creating an Internet community due to the creation of a social networking site such as Facebook or YouTube (Skinner, 2018, pp. 44–45). Web 2.0 has changed the approach to the way the web is used by adding interactions on websites, thanks to which users are able to combine, send, substitute and transfer information and knowledge and create its content together. Web 2.0 makes it possible to disseminate and create information, data and images. Undoubtedly, the evolution of the web to Web 2.0 has contributed to social changes that have directed communities to collaborate in a group. This means that technology and applications in Web 2.0 started democratic norms on the web, which is why it is often called a democratic network (Murugesan, 2010, p. 3). This network is also called people-oriented because the systems that participated in creating Web 2.0 created such opportunities as (Murugesan, 2010, p. 5):

- easy possibility to create a website and update it;
- the possibility of introducing corrections to the content published on the web;

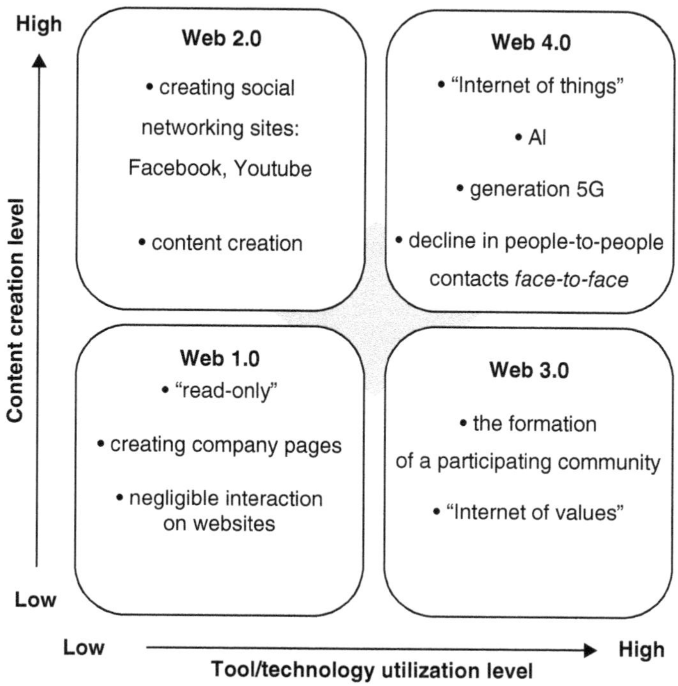

Figure 5.1 Internet evolution.
Source: Own elaboration based on: Networked Digital (2020).

- intuitive and extensive interface;
- concentrating users with common passions;
- permission to build updated applications based on existing ones on the Internet or by using data.
- In communicating with stakeholders via social media, enterprises may use various platforms, based on Web 2.0 technologies and tools, namely (Stanoevska-Slabeva, 2008, pp. 223–224):
- information Web 2.0 platforms (e.g. blogs) enabling the creation, commenting and exchange of information between Internet users;
- Internet communities (social networks) for establishing and maintaining social contacts between Internet users;
- virtual worlds that connect people with each other through their virtual representatives (called avatars) with various objects of the virtual world (an example can be Second Life).

Further transformation of the web led to the creation of Web 3.0, which made it possible to change the data, information made available on the web. Users can not only make modifications to electronic devices, but also increase the reach of the network, i.e. penetrate to a larger group of recipients of information (Noskova et al., 2017, pp. 216–17). Skinner (2016, p. 422) presents Web 3.0 as the "Internet of Values", that is, a generation based on the exchange of value, for example, the ability to control your banking and technology investments using the web. It should be mentioned that during the creation of this network, money was digitized, which made it possible to buy via the Internet using electronic money. To sum up, each user has unlimited conditions for the purchase and sale of products from anywhere in which he is located. In addition, products that are directly produced by users and sold online benefit them in material terms.

There are five breakthroughs in which Web 3.0 plays a very important role on the market and differs from previous generations, namely: data clouds, artificial intelligence, mobility, personalization and the semantic web. The aforementioned mobility of the Internet contributed to the rapid evolution of enterprises, because a large part of them not only use websites, but also the service of stakeholders has been "shifted" to devices such as mobile phones and mobile devices (Narayanan et al., 2013, p. 6). Web 3.0 works on the principle of using artificial intelligence to support systems collecting information for the user that are relevant to their needs. This is due to the intensity and amount of information appearing and the difficulty of analyzing or selecting it by users (Lubina, 2008, pp. 46–47).

The Web 4.0 generation largely uses what Web 3.0 was based on. It puts more emphasis on artificial intelligence and cloud computing. In the literature on the subject, it is believed that Web 4.0 in the future may completely integrate the real world with the virtual world. This process will be supported by the use of artificial intelligence, which will support the operation of the application and detect and fix errors in them. In addition, users will have highly developed equipment at their disposal, thanks to which they will be able to fully control data and achieve access through their authentication (Kose, 2016, p. 288).

The main idea of Web 4.0 is the development of intelligence. Created intermediaries or "agents" included in IT programmes will support the process of reasoning, communicating and cooperating with other applications or systems via the Internet, the purpose of which will be to achieve the assumed tasks on behalf of a given user (Murugesan, 2010, p. 4). Web 4.0 has also been called the Internet of Things, because more and more everyday devices have access to the Internet. The functions of the desktop computer are now taken over by laptops, smartphones and tablets. Thanks to them, you can control home appliances, such as white goods, which are already considered intelligent appliances. Nowadays, every user using the Internet provides data about himself/herself that is used by enterprises, mainly by marketers. In an era where traditional advertising methods have become ineffective, data on consumers downloaded from the Internet has gained in value. Network development offers many opportunities for enterprises, but also creates some kind of risk (Chabik, 2020).

As a result of the development of the above-mentioned networks in contemporary network communities of societies, the "culture of gift", that is of mutual giving, is experiencing a renaissance. These gifts are devoid of material or use value, they are used to build relationships. An example may be text messages, which not only help to transmit information, but mainly serve to maintain relationships between users. It is precisely on the "culture of gift" that the Internet and the digital age, as well as such phenomena as open software or file sharing services, grew (Bendyk, 2004, pp. 20–21). However, not all users engage in cooperative online activities to a varying degree. Depending on the level of activity, the following categories of users are distinguished (Li, Bernoff, 2008, pp. 41–45, Roszkowska-Menkes, 2015, p. 102; Wereda, Moch, 2020):

1. Creators – people who generate new values at least once a month, e.g. publish blog entries or online articles, run a website, upload audio–video files to the web, create new entries on Wikipedia (in the US about 25% of adult Internet users, in Europe – 15%);
2. Interlocutors – post status updates in communities and chat with others via the Internet (approx. 45% in the US, and approx. 30% in Europe);
3. Critics – a group of users who react to content generated by other Internet users, e.g. comment on blogs or Internet forums, edit Wikipedia entries, evaluate products or services (in the US – 25%, and in Europe – 20%);
4. Collectors – are users of RSS (a conventional family of markup languages for sending news and news headlines on pages selected by the user), i.e. they tag (in the USA and Europe about 10%);
5. Participants – use social networking sites (in the USA – 25%, in Europe – approx. 12%);
6. Viewers – consume content and products produced by others (in the USA – approx. 50%, and in Europe – approx. 40%);
7. Passive – do not take part in any of the above activities (in the USA – 35%, in Europe – approx. 45%).

It should be noted that the modern client has evolved since the 90s of the 20th century, when the field of computer science was close only to IT specialists and users who were able to use the network in a professional way. Now, technology is undergoing a revolution and for today's users, who increasingly identify with the word "citizen", the use of e-services has become their everyday life. Currently, mobile devices that dominate the computer market are undergoing a very significant revolution. Mobile phones have become an everyday accessory for users, just like everyday items – watches or a wallet. Now, everything can be replaced with a smartphone (Ronchi, 2019, p. 5).

On the other hand, when presenting a description of the customer's evolution over the years, it can be noticed that in the last year, the limitations resulting from the COVID-19 pandemic have meant that companies are dealing with a new, changed consumer who, by adapting to rapid changes in the environment, has developed new behaviours and habits. Some behaviours were already noticeable before, but the new conditions significantly accelerated them (remote shopping for food categories, using remote forms of entertainment and so on). Other behaviours are more timeless and long-lasting; in addition, new behaviours and shopping habits appear (remote forms of physical activity at home, remote training). Moreover, the consumer era driven by the digital transformation of individual enterprises and entire industries in the economy is entering a new stage – accelerated transformation requiring quick and agile response to customer needs, which in the new reality may change overnight. There are five types of client (KPMG Report, 2020, p. 16; Wereda, Pinzaru, 2020; Wereda, Woźniak, 2018, pp. 7–8):

1 Client 1.0 (before 1950) – a client who chose only certain groups of products, was not influenced by advertisements; had an opinion on the products and was guided by their practical application in purchasing choices; he rarely used market novelties; shaping the consumer demand was related to the use of the available production or supply capacities of the enterprise; the customer had little choice and bought products that were available and the best that could be found at the time.
2 Client 2.0 (1950–2000) – the principles of this client are still valid, but are now supported by the development of consumerism and traditional marketing; he recognizes brands and his demand for products and services is strongly driven by marketing; also uses market news advertised in the media; the first concept of the brand appeared.
3 Client 3.0 (2000–2015) – Client 1.0 and 2.0 rules are noticeable, but buyer behaviour is extended with the explosion of globalization and the Internet; for this customer, it is important to retain him with the brand through various programmes, e.g. loyalty programmes; the customer pays attention not only to the quality of the product, the brand, but also to the best customer service and individual treatment by suppliers of products and services; defines its purchasing experiences and shares them with the public; customer retention and loyalty are key aspects of the company.
4 Client 4.0 (2016–2020) – is a client whose rules (based on the experience of 1.0, 2.0 and 3.0 clients) are still evolving, but are now complicated, thanks to the huge selection, online platforms. Personal goals and creating your own personal brand outweigh marketing. It is the client who tries to influence and be influenced by other clients, it is the one who employs new ways of working and thinking; that has high expectations, where the customer journey is his or her unique journey, where companies only participate in enabling them to achieve their goals. This client is an Internet user, very demanding, well informed by electronic devices and looking for developing, competitive and innovative approaches to various challenges in various areas of life, such as banking, professional

services, automotive and IT services, healthcare, education, utilities (most aspects) and production and construction. Under the influence of the values represented by Millennials and Generation Z, Client 4.0 is a person who in his choices is more driven by personal goals and preferences and is less susceptible to mass marketing messages.

5 Customer 5.0 (from 2021) – Accelerated digitization in the time of the COVID-19 pandemic has caused customers to move to the online world, reducing the number of physical purchases in stores; self-service will dominate in many different ways and the desire for comfort and security will become more and more present in the near future; purchasing patterns change as consumers shift from unnecessary to basic spending; value and price will now be just as important as any other aspect of the experience.

Purchasing behaviour of customers during a pandemic – safety and risk

Recently, it can be noticed that the behaviour of a modern client is shaped by such factors as: increased importance of information in the lives of buyers, market saturation with goods and services, technology development, Internet access and changes in the influence of entities operating on the market (Małysa-Kaleta, 2016, pp. 144–145). Consumers of this era are autonomous people, determined to explore the market in order to obtain information, with a lot of knowledge about the market. Some of the factors help consumers to find themselves in the contemporary world that surrounds them. They are called strengths, which include such advantages as: no fear of changes, increased awareness of consumer protection, ecology, health, economy, the ability to adapt to the prevailing market conditions. Conscious and responsible consumption is an equally important advantage (Małysa-Kaleta, 2010, p. 120). In addition to these positive sides, there are also negative ones, called consumer weaknesses, and the following behaviours are attributed to them: excessive conservativeness, unconscious duplication of patterns, easy succumbing to pressure caused by global marketing activities, too hasty purchasing decisions and consumerism and prioritizing one's affairs over the rest (Małysa-Kaleta, 2016, p. 145). Recently, consumer behaviour based on the so-called 'research on-line, purchase off-line' (ROPO), which talks about searching for information about a product on the Internet before buying it in a brick-and-mortar store, has spread. It is believed that at this point every other person is going through the process. One of the arguments in favour of changing consumer behaviour is the emergence of a phenomenon called showrooming (Comarch, 2020). It is a custom that is based on searching for and assessing a product by consumers in a stationary store before using the Internet, in order to verify other products or services on the market. The most visible phenomenon is searching for the best price opportunity, which consists in analyzing prices, thanks to the Internet, and then purchasing a given product in a competing company at a price lower than what is in a stationary store. Information about the offered price of the product is important here (Gilad-Bachrach et al., 2016, p. 4). Unfortunately, the situation within a few months caused a breakthrough change affecting the basic conditions of the competitive environment that were shaped in the last years of the digital age. A high degree of uncertainty, volatility of the regulatory environment or accelerated changes in the sphere of using digital technologies create new rules of competition. Maintaining a competitive advantage and further development requires ongoing monitoring and understanding of changes in many levels of the business environment. There are many factors that currently influence the purchasing decisions of customers around the world, however, we can distinguish six basic groups, which are presented in Table 5.1.

In reference to the international research of PWC (Report PWC, 2021), the COVID-19 epidemic caused that in 2020 almost 1/3 of Poles experienced a decrease in income, while in the world, it is assumed that 40% of households experienced a decrease in income due to dismissal, loss in working hours or reducing the number of hours. In particular, it was experienced by women in the 25–44 age group, which is most likely related to the greater burden of distance teaching of children in this group. At the same time, there was an increase in household spending by 41% in the world during the pandemic on food, home heating and electricity. However, the youngest groups, aged 18–24, declare to the greatest extent that their spending related to social events has decreased. Compared to the situation in the world, Poles to a lesser extent declare both a decrease in income (Poland – 30%, the world 40%) and an increase in household spending (Poland – 30%, and the world – 41%).

According to authors from McKinsey & Company (Kohli et al., 2020, p. 1) "the period of contagion, self-isolation, and economic uncertainty has changed the way consumers behave, in some cases for many years to come". It means that many of the longer-term changes in consumer behaviour are still being formed, giving companies an opportunity to help shape the New Normal Era.[1] What is more, authors points out that present behaviour of clients has been changing in eight spheres of their lives – Figure 5.2.

The spheres that have changed from the beginning of coronavirus period:

1 Work (rise of unemployment, on-the-go consumption decline, remote working).
2 Life at home (nesting at home and surge in online).
3 Shopping and consumption (surge in e-commerce, preferences for trusted brands, decline in discretionary spending, trading down; larger baskets, reduced shopping frequency, shift to stores closer to home and the polarization of sustainability).
4 Learning (spending on learning adjacencies and remote learning).
5 Communications and information (in-person sampling decline, shift in media consumption).

Table 5.1 Factors influencing customer purchasing decisions during the pandemic

Group of factors	*Factor description*
POLITICAL	1 Government responses and extent of restrictions affecting both local and foreign markets. 2 Limited budget revenues and increased pandemic response spending. 3 Stimulating financial and economic packages. 4 Political protectionism in relation to supply chains.
ECONOMIC	1 Gross domestic product (GDP) growth forecasts. 2 The impact of isolation (lockdown) and limitations in the functioning of selected industries. 3 Fall in consumer spending. 4 Consumers focus on price–value ratio. 5 Limiting investments – priority investments in selected digital technologies. 6 Long-term economic losses for selected industries (mainly catering, travel).
SOCIAL	1 New values: environmental and social. 2 Establishing a community and a sense of belonging to a place. 3 Memories of good and bad COVID-19 experiences will impact future behaviour. 4 Less commuting, more activity at home. 5 Possible increase in unemployment, difficulties with entering the labour market, limiting manual work (acceleration of automation). 6 New employment practices, flexibility, working from home.
LEGAL, TAX, REGULATORY	1 Additional regulatory requirements related to operating in a pandemic environment. 2 Potential growth of various forms of taxation. 3 Concentration on maintaining liquidity. 4 Onshoring – supply chain protection. 5 Review of risk management processes.
TECHNOLOGICAL	1 Cybersecurity. 2 Accelerating digital transformation (automation, artificial intelligence [AI] solutions, channel integration). 3 Data integration in all systems and processes. 4 Development of Internet of Things (IoT) technology. 5 Multipoint feedback systems (information obtained at various points of contact in the Customer Journey). 6 Risk management in the supply chain.
ENVIRONMENTAL	1 Increasing importance of environmental and social aspects – the key importance of applying sustainable business practices. 2 CO^2 emission reductions resulting from reduced passenger traffic. 3 Increasing importance of localities – supporting local products and suppliers. 4 Continuation of pro-environmental activities in the field of waste management (e.g. in the field of packaging).

Source: Own elaboration based on: KPMG Report (2020).

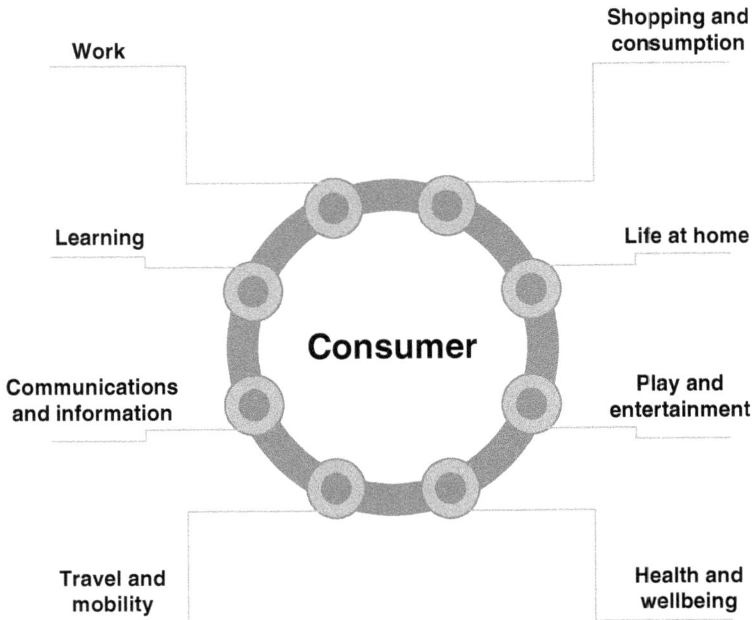

Figure 5.2 New behaviours emerging across eight areas of consumer's life.
Source: Own elaboration based on: Kohli et al. (2020, p. 2).

6 Play and entertainment (preferences for digital entertainment, entertainment channel shift, e.g. cinema to streaming and additional play time).
7 Travel and mobility (reduction in tourist spend and travel retail and increase in domestic tourism).
8 Health and mobility (focus on health and hygiene, acceleration of organic, natural, fresh, fitness on demand, e-pharmacy and e-doctor at scale).

Unfortunately, the changing technological environment and the pandemic are changing consumer behaviour, i.e. their emotions, feelings and perceptions. Modern technology has resulted in the acquisition of skills with which the consumer has not come into contact so far. Definitions such as trust, risk and safety in a person or institution have changed. Based on various consumer research conducted during the pandemic in many different markets in different regions of the world, six universal dimensions can be distinguished, the analysis of which may bring closer to the ways of functioning of the consumer, his motivation and behaviour, in particular in the perspective of changes in the new reality (KPMG Report, 2020, pp. 17–20):

1 My motivation and risk (qualities that drive behaviour and expectations). Personal risk shapes many consumer decisions. COVID-19 has

made consumers worry about the impact of transactions on their security: physical risks in stores and the potential risk of a cyber-attack when shopping online. Companies therefore need to be increasingly aware of both the factors that trigger purchasing decisions and the risk factors perceived by consumers who go through the various stages of the purchasing path. When designing an experience, remember that "protect me" must now be just as important as "know me" and "appreciate me".

2 My attention (places where we direct our attention). Companies improve their ability to focus attention on moments that are important to consumers. However, these moments have changed with the COVID-19 pandemic, as have the mechanisms by which you can get their attention. Consumers in their lives and decisions use a specific attention filter that allows them to navigate on "autopilot". It is worth noting, however, that when something significant and meaningful happens, attention is "sharpened" (e.g. hearing your name in a crowded and noisy room). The time of the COVID-19 pandemic has focused our attention and will continue to shape our understanding of what is most important to us. Consumers will be interested in things that are related to their goals, life problems and the need to satisfy their emotional needs. In such conditions, in particular, we may be more sensitive to the "persuasive" style of communication.

3 My connections (how we connect to devices, information and to each other). COVID-19 has had a significant impact on brand loyalty. Nielsen estimates that only 8% of global consumers now describe themselves as "brand loyal" (Nielsen, 2019). Increased digital interactions through search engines and paid advertising, coupled with the inherent desire for instant gratification, undermine brand loyalty. Connections take place on three levels. Firstly, the psychological relationship between the brand and its products and services; secondly, the associations we create around the brand; and thirdly, the individual links we have with its influencer network. Not only are we less convinced by brands, but we are much more influenced by the social group. Social recognition – our friends' perceptions improve our self-esteem – has become more important than simply being satisfied with the product. Loyalty to our social ties and a sense of belonging to a social group often becomes more important than brand loyalty.

4 My clock (how do we balance time constraints and how it changes in different life situations). COVID-19 has changed the way we view time. Described by some as the infinite present, it means that consumers expect the service to be provided immediately (e.g. the shortest possible delivery time for the ordered purchases). The pace of life, the growing number of incentives and the variety of digital technologies and an active lifestyle have led to what is known as "shortage", in which we feel we have less time to control. This can significantly influence our behaviour, leading us to prioritize convenience (click and pick up), speed (food

delivery) and freedom (preferring virtual over personal contact – a trend that will gain importance as virtual relationships become dominant during a pandemic). In addition, we are hungry for information, but we want it to be provided in a form that is as easy to digest as possible.

5 My portfolio (how we adjust the dynamics of expenses depending on life events). The dynamics of household spending depends primarily on the economic situation and individual life events. The time of the pandemic has introduced a high degree of uncertainty to the labour market. We observe the great importance that consumers attach to the way brands treat their employees during the pandemic. Protection of jobs is also one of the priorities of government actions in the field of subsidy programmes for entrepreneurs.
6 My safety (how safe we feel in life and at work). The time of a pandemic is also the need for consumers to switch to a remote mode of interaction with other entities and people and the employer to a much greater extent than before. It is worth bearing in mind the context in which clients using remote forms are located, e.g. those working from home can use online access to a greater extent on stationary devices; greater use of videoconferencing in remote work may translate into a greater willingness to use this communication channel in service and purchasing contacts with companies, which increases their level of safety against a pandemic. However, the mere fact of all information obtained from the media may increase the fear of getting sick, as well as cause uncertainty in relationships with others.

Research on consumer behaviour during a pandemic in Poland – own research

The subject scope of the study concerned the issue of building trust in the client–entrepreneur relationship in the digital environment, perception of digital risk by customers as well as creating their online safety. The study covered a group of 320 people who use electronic purchases, with the assumption that the respondent should make at least five purchases in electronic form within the last six months. It was assumed that the study would be conducted on a group of 20 people from all voivodeships in Poland. A random selection was used, proportional to the size of each age group in a given voivodeship (age groups: 18–20; 21–39, 40–49; 50–74 and 75 and over).

According to our research, 135 Clients 1.0, 62 Clients 2.0, 75 Clients 3.0 and 48 Clients 4.0 participated in the survey; the most diverse group of clients were people in the 21–39 age group (Table 5.2).

According to Forrester Research, the respondents were asked to define the level of their social technological ladder. Among the respondents, most people described themselves as observers (164 people). The second most numerous group are inactive people (58 people), but it should be noted

Table 5.2 Client type (by age)

Client type	*Age*					*Total*
	18–20	*21–39*	*40–49*	*50–74*	*75 and over*	
Client 1.0	9	22	20	69	15	135
Client 2.0	3	27	10	14	8	62
Client 3.0	1	35	14	23	2	75
Client 4.0	3	20	9	12	3	48

Source: Own elaboration.

that the majority of people aged 75 and over represent this level of the social technological ladder (18 out of 29 people). The smallest group are collectors – four people and critics – six people (Table 5.3).

During the survey, respondents were asked which of the indicated approaches to perceiving digital risk they identify the most with (Table 5.4).

Fifty-five percent of respondents indicated that digital risk is both a source of opportunities and a source of potential threats. Twelve percent of respondents clearly assessed digital risk as a source of potential losses, and 11% as a source of potential opportunities. In turn, as many as 22% of respondents do not analyze digital risk at all and do not think about its significance for their electronic purchases on a daily basis. The respondents were asked to rate (on a scale of 1–5) individual factors in the field of building trust in the client–company relationship, where the assessment was made of both the frequency of encountering a given factor and its importance/importance for the respondents (Table 5.5).

The trust-building factors most often encountered by the respondents were: good website of the company (3.60), positioning of the company's website in search engines (3.46), advertising in social media (3.42) and promotion of products by famous people (3.42). The least frequently respondents encountered such factors as: long-term cooperation based on personal contact (2.28) and a large number of contacts and concluded contracts in a short period (2.72). The study showed that the most important factors of building trust in client–entrepreneur relations include: good website of the company (3.82), minimizing the risk of transactions in the long term (3.58) and loyalty programmes (3.52). The least important factors are: personal contacts and acquaintances (2.96) and a large number of contacts and contracts concluded in a short period (3.02). During the survey, respondents were asked to indicate the level of consent to the indicated data protection and privacy statements in the case of online purchases. In the case of defining digital risk, the majority of respondents defined it as a source of both threats (losses) and opportunities (potential benefits) – Table 5.6.

Research shows that 51% of respondents believe that online stores process personal data in a lawful and transparent manner, ensuring fairness towards individuals. Thirty-two percent of respondents do not agree with

Table 5.3 The level of the social technological ladder of the respondents (by age)

The level of the social technological ladder	*Age*					*Total*
	18–20	*21–39*	*40–49*	*50–74*	*75 and over*	
Creator (publishes blogs and websites monthly, uploads videos he has created, uploads audio or music you've created, writes articles or stories, and publishes them online)	3	8	5	7	3	26
Interlocutor (weekly status updates on the social network, post updates, e.g. on Twitter or chat with others via the Internet)	2	15	5	7	0	29
Critic (monthly reviews of posts and/or reviews of products or services, comments on someone else's blog, participation in online forums and editing articles on Wikipedia)	0	1	2	3	0	6
Collector (monthly uses RSS feeds [a conventional family of markup languages to send news headlines and news on user-selected RSS pages], votes for online websites, adds "tags" to websites or photos)	0	2	1	0	1	4
Participant (monthly maintains a profile on a social networking site and visits social networking sites)	2	6	7	15	3	33
Observer (they consume content and products produced by others, i.e. reads blogs monthly, listens to podcasts, watches videos from other users, reads online forums, customer ratings/reviews and tweets)	8	67	27	58	4	164
Inactive (does not participate in any of the above activities)	1	5	6	28	18	58

Source: Own elaboration.

this statement. Seventeen percent of respondents are indifferent to the processing of their personal data by online stores. Fifty-one percent of respondents believe that online stores have specific data processing purposes and indicate these purposes to individuals when collecting their personal data. Twenty-eight percent of respondents are of the opposite opinion. For 21%

Table 5.4 Digital risk perception

Digital risk perception	*No. of answers*	*Percentage*
Digital risk as a source of threats (potential losses)	38	12
Digital risk as a source of both threats (losses) and opportunities (potential benefits)	176	55
Digital risk mainly as a source of opportunities (potential benefits)	35	11
I do not analyze digital risk and I do not think about its significance for my electronic purchases on a daily basis.	71	22

Source: Own elaboration.

Table 5.5 Factors building trust in client–entrepreneur relations

Factors building trust	*The frequency of the customer's contact with a given factor*	*Importance/ importance of a given factor for the client*
Received discounts during long-term cooperation	3.12	3.33
Minimizing the transaction risk in the long run	2.98	3.58
The prestige and brand of the company (the company's reputation on the market)	3.30	3.46
Personal contacts and acquaintances	2.93	2.96
Long-term cooperation based on personal contact	2.28	3.08
A large number of contacts and concluded contracts in a short period of time	2.72	3.02
Mutual loyalty	3.21	3.51
Influence of the environment, e.g. media opinions on the company's reputation, good public relations, etc.	3.41	3.48
Positioning the website in search engines	3.46	3.49
Social media advertising	3.42	3.39
Promoting products by famous people	3.42	3.08
Good business website	3.60	3.82
Loyalty programmes	3.33	3.52

Source: Own elaboration.

Table 5.6 The level of consent to the indicated statements regarding the protection of personal data and privacy when making online purchases

I am sure that online stores:	*Consent level (%)*				
	I strongly disagree	*I disagree a bit*	*I do not care*	*I agree a little*	*I strongly agree*
Process personal data in a lawful and transparent manner, ensuring fairness towards natural persons.	11	21	17	31	20
Have specific data processing purposes and indicate these purposes to individuals when collecting their personal data.	8	20	21	30	21
They collect and process only the personal data that is necessary to achieve the sales purpose.	9	21	22	22	26
Ensure that personal data is accurate and up-to-date, taking into account the purposes for which it is processed, and correct it if not.	7	20	22	32	19
Ensure that personal data is kept for no longer than is necessary for the purposes for which it was collected.	9	19	18	35	19
Install appropriate technical and organizational security measures to ensure the security of personal data, including protection against unauthorized or unlawful processing and accidental loss, destruction or damage, using appropriate technology.	7	17	24	27	25
In special cases, personal data is stored for a longer period for archiving purposes in the public interest or for scientific or historical research reasons, provided that appropriate technical and organizational measures are taken.	11	12	25	36	16
Ensure that the data stored is accurate and up-to-date.	7	19	22	34	18

Source: Own elaboration.

of respondents, the indicated issue did not matter. Forty-eight percent of respondents believe that online stores collect and process only the personal data that is necessary to achieve the sales goal, but 30% believe that these stores also collect and process data that is not necessary for the purchase and sale transaction. For 22% of respondents, this issue is indifferent. More than half of the respondents (51%) indicated that online stores ensure that personal data is accurate and up-to-date, taking into account the purposes for which it is processed, and correct it if it is not. The opposite opinion is shared by 27% of respondents. The issue of up-to-date data processed by online stores is irrelevant for 22% of respondents. As many as 54% of respondents believe that online stores ensure that personal data is stored no longer than necessary for the purposes for which it was collected. Twenty-eight percent of the respondents have a different opinion. For 18% of respondents, this issue is not important. Fifty-two percent of respondents believe that online stores install appropriate technical and organizational security measures to ensure the security of personal data, including protection against unauthorized or unlawful processing and accidental loss, destruction or damage, using appropriate technology. Twenty-four percent of the respondents have the opposite opinion. The survey results show that 52% of respondents believe that in special cases personal data is stored by online stores for a longer period for archiving purposes in the public interest or for scientific or historical research reasons, provided that appropriate technical and organizational measures are put in place. Twenty-three percent of respondents have a different opinion. For 25% of respondents, this issue is irrelevant. Fifty-four percent of respondents believe that online stores ensure that the data stored is accurate and up-to-date. Twenty-six percent of the respondents are of the opposite opinion. The issue of timeliness and accuracy of data stored and processed by online stores does not matter for 22% of respondents.

Research shows that online shoppers feel relatively safe. About half of them believe that online stores ensure the security of the personal data they provide. About 25% of respondents are of the opposite opinion. What is puzzling, however, is the level of indifference of customers shopping online. For each of the statements it fluctuated at the level of 25%. This shows that the respondents are not interested in how the personal data they provide are processed (Wereda, Moch, 2020).

Conclusions

The customer experience through COVID-19 has been changing all over the world because everybody is facing new types of changes. The changes that provide positive experiences are likely to last longer, particularly those driven by convenience and well-being, such as digital adoption, value-based purchasing and increased health awareness. This provides an opportunity for firms to offer innovative, modular, granular, value-based and integrated products to meet customer needs. Moreover, a modern customer is a person who is characterized by several elements:

- they need safety in life and care in the market;
- want to minimize the risk associated with stationary and online purchases;
- need market personalization;
- want to have a positive experience of contacting companies when living remotely.

Note

1 **New Normal Era** can be defined as time after the coronavirus period.

References

Adamczewski, P. (2018). Organizacja data-driven w ewolucji transformacji cyfrowej. *Prace Naukowe Uniwersytetu Ekonomicznego we Wrocławiu*, 527.
Bendyk, E. (2004). *Antymatrix. W labiryncie sieci.* Warszawa: WAB.
Chabik, J. (2020). *Internet rzeczy – rewolucja tuż za rogiem.* www.ican.pl.
Comarch (2020). *Konsument digitalny w epoce wielokanałowej sprzedaży.* www.comarch.pl.
Gilad-Bachrach, R. et al. (2016). Crypto Nets: Applying Neural Networks to Encrypted Data with High through Put and Accuracy. *International Conference on Machine Learning*, New York.
Kelly, K. (1995). *Out of Control, The New Biology of Machines, Social Systems & the Economic World.* New York: Basic Books.
Kohli, S., Timelin, B., Fabius, V. and Veranen, S.V. (2020). *How COVID-19 Is Changing Consumer Behavior – Now and Forever.* France: McKinsey&Company.
Kose, U. (2016). *Ideas on the Future of Intelligent Web-Based E-Learning*, In: Kose, U. and Durmus, K. (Eds.), *Artificial Intelligence Applications in Distance Education.* Harshey: IGI Global.
Li, C. and Bernoff, J. (2008). *Groundswell. Winning in a World Transformed by Social Technologies.* Boston, MA: Harvard Business Press.
Lubina, E. (2008). Web 3.0 jako transgresja kulturowa o wymiarze społecznym. *e-Mentor*, 1(23).
Małysa-Kaleta, A. (2010). *Kierunki oraz determinanty przemian konsumpcji w Polsce i Czechach na tle procesów integracji europejskiej.* Katowice: Uniwersytet Ekonomiczny w Katowicach.
Małysa-Kaleta, A. (2016). Misja konsumenta we współczesnym świecie. *Handel Wewnętrzny*, 4.
Murugesan, S. (2010). *Handbook of Research on Web 2.0, 3.0 and X.O: Technologies, Business, and Social Applications.* New York: Information Science Reference.
Narayana, V.K. and Colarelli O'Connor, G. (2010). *Encyclopaedia of Technology and Innovation Management.* Malden, MA: Wiley Blackwell Publishing.
Narayanan, A., Narayan, N. and Sathyan, S. (2013). *A Comprehensive Guide to Enterprise Mobility.* Abingdon: CRC Press, Taylor & Francis Group.

Networked Digital (2020). *Model ewolucji Internetu: wersja 3.0*. www.networkeddigital.com.

Nielsen (2019). *Consumer Disloyalty Is the New Normal*. www.nielsen.com/eu.

Noskova, T., Pavlova T. and Yakovleva, O. (2017). Electronic Communication in Education: A Study of New Opportunities. *Simulation and Communication 'DLSC 2017'*, University of Defence, Brno.

Report "13 faktów o transformacji cyfrowej…czyli wszystko co chciałbyś wiedzieć o cyfryzacji, ale bałeś się zapytać. Digital Shapers" (2021). www.digitalpoland.org.

Report "World Intellectual Property Indicators 2019" (2019). Geneva: World Intellectual Property Organization.

Report KPMG "Doświadczenia klientów w nowej rzeczywistości" (2020). www.kpmg.pl.

Report PWC "Nowy obraz polskiego konsumenta. Postawy i zachowania Polaków w obliczu pandemii koronawirusa" (2021). www.pwc.pl.

Ronchi, A.M. (2019). *e-Citizens: Toward a New Model of (Inter)active Citizenry*. Cham: Springer Nature.

Roszkowska-Menkes, M. (2015). *Open Innovations: Finding Balance*. Warsaw: SGH.

Shirky, C. (2010). *Cognitive Surplus: Creativity and Generosity in a Connected Age*. New York: The Penguin Press.

Skinner, C. (2016). *Value Web. How Fintech Firms Are Using Mobile and Blockchain Technologies to Create the Internet of Value*. Singapore: Marshall Cavendish Business.

Skinner, C. (2018). *Cyfrowi Ludzie. Nasza Czwarta Rewolucja*. Warszawa: Poltex.

Stanoevska-Slabeva, K. (2008). *Die Potenziale des Web 2.0 für das Interaktive Marketing*, In: Belz, C., Schögel, M., Arndt, O. and Walter, W. (Eds.), *Interaktives Marketing. Neue Wege zum Dialog mit Kunden*. Wiesbaden: Gabler Verlag.

Wereda, W. and Moch, N. (2020). *The Role of the Digital Customer in the Contemporary Market. Aspects of Trust, Risk, and Safety*. In: Constantin, B., Zbuchea, A., Anghel, F. and Hrib, B. (Eds.), *Strategica 2020. Preparing for Tomorrow, Today*. Bucharest: Tritonic Publishing House.

Wereda, W. and Pinzaru, F. (2020). Net Generation's Customer Experience during a Pandemic. *Nowoczesne Systemy Zarządzania*, 15(3), 63–74.

Wereda, W. and Woźniak, J. (2019). Building Relationships with Customer 4.0 in the Era of Marketing 4.0: The Case Study of Innovative Enterprises in Poland. *Social Sciences*, 8(6), 2–27.

6 Using the potential of the ISO 9001:2015 and ISO 22301:2019 standards in the fight against COVID-19

Małgorzata Dąbrowska-Świder

Introduction

There have been many instances of pandemic outbreaks in history and their disastrous consequences for mankind, such as the Black Death in medieval Europe that took a huge death toll. But no one could imagine that in our times when people are flying to the moon, exploring the farthest corners of space and descending to the bottom of the Marian Trench, something like this could happen. Scientists, doctors, economists, politicians and everyone who cares about the well-being of their own country, and the entire planet, have to rise to the challenge. At this point, we are already a few steps ahead compared to the situation in which the world found itself at the first stage of the outbreak of the SARS-COV-2 coronavirus. However, we are still making small steps instead of great leaps. Teams of virology scientists are working day and night to help patients get over this dangerous disease, whose consequences we will have to face for many years to come. And this is not only about the protection of human health and life. The response to COVID-19 has also had a disastrous impact on many branches of the economy, industry and sometimes the entire structure of countries. The expected reaction of every citizen is to look towards state leaders and the government to come up with systemic solutions in the field of what may be broadly understood as sense of security. The daily news from all over the world gives few reasons for optimism. Far from it, it triggers fear in people and leads to irrational behaviour, with consequences that cannot be predicted at present and may only become apparent in the near future. This particularly applies to the younger generation and children. It can already be said that people have started to perceive their lives in the context of "before the pandemic/after the pandemic" or "before the 'masks'/after the 'masks'". Until the outbreak of COVID-19, such a turning point of reference for many people in Europe was the time before and after the Second World War, especially among the generation of our parents and grandparents. This is why it is crucial to strive to return to normal everyday life. What was definitely lacking at the beginning of the pandemic were systemic and effective measures on the part of the European Union, as no one had made a risk analysis taking such

DOI: 10.4324/9781003285717-6

circumstances into account. There are various types of insurance and protective measures against cataclysms, available to individuals, companies or organizations, but no one has thought about the possibility of such a serious threat in the form of a severe contagious disease, at a global level. Single-handed actions taken by the governments of individual countries showed the possible consequences of a lack of unanimity in terms of boosting the level of security of the EU member states. Each country adopted its own scenario in this regard, although they could have drawn from the experience of countries that had been at the front line in the battle against COVID-19 at the beginning of the pandemic. In recent months, new solutions have been adopted by the European Council and the European Commission in this regard. Almost every day, we can hear about new initiatives in various areas in terms of fighting the consequences of the pandemic. On 11 September 2020, the Council agreed to add EUR 6.2 billion to the EU 2020 budget to address the impact of the COVID-19 crisis. The revised budget provides increased funds for the development of a vaccine and its distribution. The European Commission will use these funds to order the vaccine (EUR 1.09 billion), as well as allocating money for Coronavirus Response Investment Initiatives (basic initiative and initiative+). The money from the EU budget will also be used to fight the crisis caused by COVID-19 (EUR 5.1 billion) (https://www.consilium.europa.eu/pl/policies/coronavirus/). On 24 September 2020, the European Centre for Disease Prevention and Control (ECDC) updated its Rapid Risk Assessment for the development of the epidemiological situation. Due to the increase in the number of infections throughout the UK as well as Europe, and the upward trend of the infection rate, it called for tougher restrictions. On 8 October 2020, the European Commission approved a third contract with the pharmaceutical company Janssen Pharmaceutica NV for the purchase of a potential vaccine that was in Phase III of clinical trials for 200 million people and another 200 million doses to be purchased by individual member states. The Commission also signed a contract with Gilead for 500,000 doses of remdesivir – the only drug with a conditional marketing authorization in the European Union for the treatment of COVID-19 patients who require supplemental oxygen. On 13 October 2020, EU member states settled on a coordinated approach to travel restrictions due to the pandemic, based on the classification of regions into various zones (green, orange, red and grey) depending on the local epidemiological situation. This approach involved a timely provision of information for travelers and lifting restrictions (e.g. compulsory quarantine or tests) for those arriving from "green" zones. On 15 October 2020, the European Commission's Communication on Preparedness for COVID-19 vaccination strategies and vaccine deployment was announced, which requires individual member states to identify priority groups that should receive the vaccine first once it becomes available. On 19 October 2020, the so-called interoperability gateway was launched. It is an EU-wide system created at the request of EU member states in order to ensure mutual communication for contact tracing and warning apps. The system currently includes applications used by countries such as Germany, Ireland and Italy, with Russian, Czech, Danish and Latvian apps scheduled to be added next week, and others later in November 2020. This form of communication is currently used by 30 million people, which is the equivalent of two thirds of all downloaded applications within the EU (https://ec.europa.eu/info/live-work-travel-eu/health/coronavirus-response_pl#euactions). On 26 May 2020, the European Commission came up with a key initiative involving a comprehensive recovery plan for Europe, with full use of the EU budget, aimed at offsetting the economic and social losses caused by the pandemic, reviving the European economy and preserving existing jobs. The initiative comprises two solutions: Next Generation – EUR 750 billion to be added to the EU budget in 2021–2024, as well as targeted reinforcements to the long-term EU budget for 2021–2027, which will amount in total to EUR 1.85 trillion (https://ec.europa.eu/info/live-work-travel-eu/health/coronavirus-response/recovery-plan-europe_pl). No one can predict how long the world will have to deal with the consequences of the pandemic, but one thing is certain, the fight with this terrible disease will be neither easy nor quick. This is why it is important to take actions in each area, at each level, starting from supranational structures such as the EU or the World Health Organization, through measures taken by the governments of individual countries, to locally implemented solutions. This brings to mind the slogan "act globally, think locally", which is the reversal of the popular saying. Yoko Ishikura describes this principle, emphasizing that the more global the approach of a given company is, the more important it becomes to collect and process information from individual local markets. The collection of such data allows for the preparation of an appropriate range of products, the right marketing strategy and, above all, the optimal design of the value chain layout (Ishikura, 2007). The purpose of this article is not to evaluate the adopted solutions and to consider what health, economic, social and cultural consequences the pandemic will have in the near future, but to try to analyze whether certain measures can be undertaken by an organization with an implemented management system based on ISO 22301:2019 and 9001:2015.

Normative solutions as the key to the efficient operation of an organization and a guarantee of its own well-being, as well as the well-being of the environment in which it functions

Every organization, however small, functions in a specific environment. Its scope is determined by the nature of the organization, its purpose and activities. All members of a given organization should be aware that defining the context of its operation is of key significance and has a direct or indirect impact on the operation of the organization (Griffin, 1997). A significant advantage of ISO standards is certain common elements and requirements, which are defined almost identically. Both ISO 22301:2019 and ISO 9001:2015 have such common elements. These include points 4 to 7 as well as 9 and 10. Point 8 is specific to each of the standards and reflects its nature and distinctiveness. As regards the requirements of point 4 for both standards, apart from all the elements determining the development and business approach, attention should also be paid to the immediate environment. The standards offer a whole range of possibilities to create an appropriate mechanism that would make it possible to respond to changes in the environment of the organization in a flexible manner. An example of such a change is the recent outbreak of the coronavirus and the need to comply with new legal requirements introduced as a response to the situation by state authorities of individual countries, in order to protect the health and life of their citizens. In terms of an organization, these changes forced the adoption of internal instructions related to everyday functioning. Each organization featuring quality management and business continuity management is an efficiently operating system, consisting of a number of interconnected elements. Each has its own objectives, which together make for the success of the whole organization (Hopej, Kral, 2011). Before the outbreak of the pandemic, such elements were not taken into account when identifying possible risks, not only nationally but also in terms of an organization. Such a way of thinking is best evidenced by the fact that the rank of specialists in infectious diseases working in infectious wards in Poland includes 367 working age physicians, 42 retirement age physicians and 80 postgraduate training physicians, which gives a total of 479 specialists (based on the data of the Polish Society of Epidemiologists and Doctors of Infectious Diseases: http://www.pteilchz.org.pl/). This proves that infectious diseases were not considered as a critical element of threat in the model of the contemporary world, with its prevailing assumptions that the level of development of modern medicine is sufficient to deal with any infection. On top of that, for many years, this specialization has been quite unpopular among students of medicine, who feared they would not be able to find a job, and instead tended to choose "safe" specializations – in terms of the labour market – like GP. If someone has taken part in fire training at least once, he or she understands well the meaning and purpose of such actions and can quickly evacuate. Japan is an excellent example of preparedness for crisis situations that may pose a threat to human health and life at any time. In this case, we refer to earthquakes. Like no other country in the world, Japan is perfectly prepared in terms of crisis management. Even young children regularly undergo earthquake preparation drills and learn a number of rules and modes of behaviour that they internalize for the rest of their lives. Another example of how Japan manages the risks inherent due to its geographical location is the adoption of special architecture and the use of the latest technologies protecting against seismic shocks. For years, the Japanese state authorities have also been considering a solution that would guard the coasts from giant tsunami waves. In 2015, Japan unveiled plans to build a high wall that would keep the country's coastline safe from the devastating force of the sea. According to

"The Independent", the structure will be 250 miles long, and in some places 12.5 m high. The media also reports that the cost of the project is expected to reach $6.8 billion. The wall will be made of cement and will consist of smaller breakwater structures connected to each other. This will facilitate the construction process. "The Independent" emphasizes that the tsunami that struck the coast of Japan in March 2011 as a result of the most powerful earthquake in history produced waves up to 40 m high. According to preliminary estimates, the total costs incurred by Japan due to that natural disaster amounted to around USD 34 billion (https://wiadomosci.onet.pl/swiat/the-independent-japonia-wybuduje-swoj-wielki-mur/k1gjtw). The consequences of the earthquake and the gigantic tsunami that hit Japan in March 2011 are still felt to this day, as the worst natural disaster in Japan since the war was accompanied by a nuclear accident at the Fukushima power plant, where the cooling systems failed, resulting in the fuel rods melting. This led to the emission of radioactive substances. The Fukushima Daiichi nuclear disaster was the largest disaster of this kind since the reactor explosion in Chernobyl in 1986. When the SARS-COV-2 pandemic was globally announced, it was not clear what kind of threat the world would have to deal with. Every day new information is provided, mainly through the local and global media, expanding people's knowledge base about this phenomenon. This enables an appropriate classification of possible threats and assess what impact they are likely to have on the operation of one's organization, as well as to develop a whole set of measures to ensure the safety of the employees (including meeting the requirements of point 6.1 of ISO 9001:2015 and ISO 22301:2019). Therefore, it is necessary to consider developing and implementing certain routine courses of action in terms of health and safety of all employees in the face of the threats posed by the pandemic. This type of approach is reasonable in the context of the functioning of any organization at present, but it will certainly also be useful in case similar threats arise in the future. In addition, it will also facilitate solving other problems. As an example, it is worth citing one of the Spanish companies operating in Poland, which recommends that its employees use disinfectants and wear masks, as well as conducts training in the principles of the new sanitary regime both at work and outside work. They have also issued recommendations regarding commuting to and from work and prohibited their employees and families from leaving their place of residence during their vacation. Such guidelines and recommendations prove that the perception of the context of the organization's environment plays a key role in the introduction of specific restrictions. Extending such restrictions to family members of the employees has an additional positive impact in terms of increasing the number of people trained and made aware in this regard. Such measures could have been initially regarded as actions violating personal freedom – all the more so since they had been introduced much earlier than nation-wide restrictions imposed due to the rapid spread of the virus. They only came to be appreciated by the employees of the organization in question and their families later and allowed for a better understanding of subsequent actions taken by the Polish government. This example shows how effective solutions introduced at the organizational level can positively affect the environment of the organization. The effectiveness of such simple solutions is undoubtedly the best guarantee of security. If one assumes that most people spend more time at work and on their way to work (at least this was the case so far), then the sense of security provided in terms of the organization is of great importance for every employee, as well as his or her immediate surroundings – family and friends. In this way, the sense of security is strengthened in an analogous way to the phenomenon of connected vessels. Perhaps it would be reasonable to take advantage of this method. Kevin W. Knight – Chairman of the ISO Working Group, which developed the ISO 31000 risk management standard – stated that “all organizations, regardless whether large or small, are faced with internal and external factors that cause uncertainty. The result of this uncertainty is risk, which is inherent in all types of activities”. In many companies and organizations, the purchase of insurance had been a widely accepted and practiced method of protection against risk. However, the increasing costs of insurance policies became an obstacle. Consequently, people started to seek out other ways of dealing with risk, such as avoiding it in the first place by refraining from activities with a high level of responsibility or by reducing the responsibility involved. The current situation related to the global pandemic, however, requires specific actions to minimize its negative consequences (Wróblewski, 2011). The application of Business Continuity Management (BCM) can be an excellent tool for this purpose. It represents a holistic management concept aimed at determining the potential impact of disruptions to an organization and creating conditions for building resilience to them and improving the ability to effectively protect the interests of the owners, reputation and brand of the organization as well as the values it holds (definition of The Business Institute). Including risk management in the ISO standards turned out to be a successful measure, but – as shown in the examples above – it was insufficient. Risk management is aimed at providing protection and security, but it refers to threats and opportunities. It is fortunate that the aspects related to risks have started to be treated more seriously by organizations. The collection of the data required for risk management, an analysis of the context of the organization and the resources, setting goals, defining the scope of the system, risk assessment methodology, reporting and communication as well as an analysis of the collected data ensure a higher level of security for each organization that has adopted the above-mentioned measures. Furthermore, the implementation of the ISO 22301:2019 standard additionally supports the functioning of mechanisms related to the need for developing recovery plans, which can be used to mitigate disruptions in business operations and enable the organization to return to normal functioning. Therefore, a combination of business continuity management and risk management systems presents an ideal solution that can enable each organization to identify potential threats, prevent disaster, develop procedures to minimize the consequences of such events for the organization, its environment and stakeholders as well as figure out various options to restore the normal operation of the organization.

Adoption of ISO 9001:2015 and ISO 22301:2019 as a protective measure in the fight against COVID-19

A good reference point for introducing new normative solutions regarding ISO 9001:2015 and ISO 22301:2019 aimed at increasing the level of an organization's security is Section 7 Support. Its individual subsections leave room for new solutions. Starting from 7.1 Resources, simply and with little effort, new procedures or instructions can be introduced regarding the supplementation of internal resources with additional personal protective equipment in the event of an epidemiological emergency to be provided for the organization's employees and – in an extended version – to its customers too. On the basis of their current experience, each organization is able to determine the size of its basic reserves, which should be maintained in order to react quickly to changes and run a trouble-free operation. In this case, the term "resources" does not only concern material aspects, but is also closely related to the people employed, whose appropriate competences are a guarantee of the effectiveness of the organization's operation (Oleksyn, 1997). If there is a need to constantly maintain a high level of responsiveness, one should consider employing or establishing permanent cooperation with a specialist who will handle the process of training and make all employees aware of epidemiological safety rules on an ongoing basis (Subsection 7.1.2. of the ISO 9001 and 7.2 ISO 22301 standard). In addition, one should ensure that all legal regulations and requirements are met in this respect. Each organization maintains such a level of infrastructure as is required for its proper functioning (Subsection 7.1.3 of the ISO 9001 and 7.2 ISO 22301 standard). There have been numerous examples of bottom-up initiatives reported in the media, where organizations, using the available resources and technologies, were able to quickly shift their production to produce, for instance, ventilators, disinfecting products, personal protective equipment such as face masks, face shields, disposable gloves, protective clothing and aprons. At the early stage of a pandemic, it suddenly became apparent that all the countries affected by the pandemic were lacking sufficient amounts of almost all the necessary types of personal protective equipment. The crisis that ensued affected each country so severely that due to the fear of being unable to secure their own supplies, mutual aid in this regard was abandoned. This catastrophic situation was additionally exacerbated by the virtual monopoly of a single global producer and contributed to disruptions in the supply chain. Fortunately, this was only a temporary predicament which most countries have now started to overcome. If appropriate system solutions were introduced in terms of operation of individual organizations in accordance with the requirements of ISO 9001 and ISO 22301, the situation would certainly be easier to control. As regards Subsection 7.1.4 of ISO 9001:2015, which defines the environment for the functioning of processes, the mere adoption of additional protective measures by an organization has a positive impact on the emotional state of the employees and their families, which in turn increases their sense of security. The key importance of protecting human health and life imposes the obligation to include such measures and processes that are necessary for the effectiveness of the organization's management systems within appropriate documentation (Subsection 7.5 of ISO 9001 and ISO 22301). Such documentation should list a description of the competences of the employees and the scope of their responsibilities in terms of implementing individual processes. Fostering awareness among employees (Subsection 7.3 of ISO 9001 and ISO 22301) always seems to be a daunting task at the beginning. This is mainly due to the negative attitude of the majority of participants in this process, who, fearing that they may have to face new challenges and subsequent changes, adopt a defensive attitude. However, after breaking the initial ice, the benefits of such solutions become apparent and prove invaluable. Many common areas of the ISO group of standards can have a much wider application for the protection of common values and a sense of security, not to mention such additional positive aspects as: standardization of documentation, time and cost efficiency, simplification of measures taken, etc.

Vietnam and Mongolia as examples of countries who have adopted systemic, effective actions

The phenomenon of Vietnam has rarely been publicly discussed. This country, which borders China and has 97 million inhabitants, gave an example to the rest of the world on how to cope with the pandemic. First of all, the response of the Vietnamese state authorities was quick and extremely drastic. As early as the beginning of January, before any case had been reported in the country (and only two people had died in Wuhan), the Vietnamese government took a number of important steps. It closed its border with China, introduced travel restrictions and close monitoring of borders, while also increasing the number of coronavirus tests in many places. For the Lunar New Year, schools were closed and were opened again only in mid-May 2020. According to Dr Todd Pollack of Harvard's Partnership for Health Advancement, who works in the capital of Vietnam, Hanoi, and Professor Guy Thwaites of the Clinical Research Unit of the University of Oxford in Ho Chi Minh, the swift actions taken by the Vietnamese government looked like an overreaction at the beginning of the year, but over time they proved to have been sensible. The reason why the Vietnamese approach proved so effective is also the fact that the country had to deal with SARS in 2003, bird flu in 2010 and outbreaks of measles and tropical dengue disease previously. As of 17 May 2020, Vietnam had only 320 cases of COVID-19, including 260 recoveries and no deaths. Vietnam's approach taught the whole world a valuable lesson (https://tech.wp.pl/wietnam-kraj-ktory-dokonal-cudu-97-mln-mieszkancow-i-nikt-nie-zmarl-na-koronawirusa-6511565432289409a). In addition to Vietnam, there is another Asian country that boasts a very low number of coronavirus infections – Mongolia, where the number of deaths from COVID-19 remains zero, despite the fact that the country only borders Russia and China (its border with China is the longest land border in the world). According to research done by Davaadorj Rendoo, an epidemiologist based in Ulan Bator, one of the reasons Mongolia managed to avoid the crisis related to COVID-19 was its early and centralized response to the pandemic. In Mongolia, the first news about a new virus spreading in China was reported around New Year's Day. On 10 January, the first public statement was issued, which introduced the obligation to cover the mouth and nose in public. Mongolia has a poor healthcare system and lacks enough ventilators. In addition, the country has a harsh, dry and cold climate with seasonal influenza outbreaks from November to February. Therefore, emphasis was placed on effectively preventing the spread of the disease. A significant advantage in this case was the country's small population (about 3.2 million people). Mongolia received testing kits from the World Health Organization, which it put to use very quickly. The first case of COVID-19 was a French citizen working in Mongolia who was diagnosed on 9 March. The country's borders were closed and the Ministry of Health started to hold information meetings on a daily basis to monitor the situation on an ongoing basis (https://300gospodarka.pl/news/koronawirus-mongolia-nie-ma-zadnej-ofiary-smiertelnej).

The examples of these two Asian countries prove the extreme self-discipline of their citizens, who can patiently sit out all the inconveniences resulting from the introduced restrictions, as well as their mindset focused on achieving goals for the common good, which in this case was to stop the spread of the pandemic. The literature on the subject often mentions the Japanese organizational culture, where all members of a given organization are identified with its goals. According to Francis Fukuyama: "the ability to cooperate with others depends on the scope of acceptance of the standards in force within the organization, as well as the importance of the common good" (Fukujama, 1997, p. 20). Thus, prioritizing the common good over individual interests in the organization can make each of its members more willing to become involved in achieving the organization's success as a whole. Such an attitude developed over a long time yields measurable results. Right now we are witnessing a great change and the development of mechanisms of solidarity and social responsibility. The grassroots initiatives that are being implemented in many European countries, including Poland, are reflected in a survey conducted during 22–26 June 2020, after the first wave of the pandemic. Fifty-two people took part, aged between 19 and 23 years old. Around 78.8% were women (41 respondents) and 21.2% were men (11 respondents).

The majority of the people surveyed (38.5% – 20 people) lived in cities with a population of over 500,000 people, followed by inhabitants of rural areas (30.8% – 16 people) and towns of up to 50,000 inhabitants (28.8% – 15 people). One person surveyed lived in a city with a population of less than 500,000 people. When asked whether they were monitoring the current epidemiological situation in the country and around the world, 48.1% answered affirmatively (5.8% – three respondents: definitely yes, 42.3% – 22 respondents: rather yes), while 51.9% answered negatively (44.2% – 23 respondents: rather not, 7.7% – four respondents: definitely not). As regards covering the mouth and nose in public places, 48.1% (25 respondents) were definitely in favour of such measures, 36.5% (19 respondents) – rather in favour, and 15.4% (eight respondents) were rather against them. None of the respondents was definitely against such preventive measures. When asked about the 2-m social distancing rule, 13.5% (seven respondents) were definitely in favour, 50% (26 respondents) – rather in favour, while 30.8% (16 respondents) were rather against it and 5.8% (three respondents) – definitely against it. Around 65.4% of the respondents (34 people) confirmed that they spend at least 30 seconds washing their hands, while 34.6% (18 people) denied doing so. The crisis related to the pandemic caused 19.2% of the respondents (ten people) to lose their jobs, while 80.8% (42 people) were able to keep their jobs. According to 36.5% of the respondents (19 people), the pandemic did not have a negative impact on their physical activity (at least 30 minutes, at least five days a week), but 63.5% of the respondents (33 people) claimed that the pandemic and the restrictions imposed to curb it turned out to be a clear obstacle in this regard. Regarding the question concerning restrictions in movement, 96.2% of the respondents (50 people) answered that the pandemic has definitely limited their freedom of movement (48.1% – definitely yes, 48.1% – rather yes), while only 3.8% (two people) answered it has not really had such an impact. In terms of the impact of the pandemic on social life, 40.4% of the respondents (21 people) answered that the pandemic has had a negative impact on their contacts with friends (7.7% – four people: definitely yes, 32.7% – 17 people: rather yes), while 59.65% denied that the pandemic has had any impact on their relationships with other people (44.2% – 23 people: rather no, 15.4% – eight people: definitely no). For 56.3% of the respondents (27 people), their greatest concern during the pandemic was if they or their family members would contract COVID-19. Twenty-five percent (12 people) feared the collapse of the health system, 41.7% (20 people) were afraid of a deterioration of their relationships with other people and loneliness. Around 52.1% of the respondents (25 people) were concerned about another wave of the pandemic and the further spread of the virus, while others indicated other concerns, such as losing their job or inflation (6.3% – three people). When asked about general well-being during the pandemic, 5.8% of the respondents (three people) answered that it was great, 71.2% (37 people) assessed it as quite good, while others 21.2% (11 people) as rather bad. Only one respondent assessed his well-being as definitely terrible during the pandemic. The greatest support for 76.9% of the respondents (40 people) were their closest family, relatives and friends. Around 9.6% (five people) considered their passion as the best source of support. Around 5.8% (three people) were happy with being alone all by themselves, while social media turned out to be a support for 3.8% of the respondents (two people). The remaining people chose to answer "other" as their sources of support. Regarding active involvement in the fight against the coronavirus, 5.8% of the respondents (three people) answered they were helping by sewing masks, 3.8% (two people) made donations to a cause, 9.6% (five people) recorded #Hot16challenge and 7.7% (four people) assisted local seniors with their shopping. Unfortunately, as many as 84.6% of the respondents (44 people) focused instead on their own safety and the safety of their family, and 3.8% (two people) did not support any form of activity in terms of fighting the effects of the pandemic. The data shows how much still needs to be done in terms of building systemic solutions, starting from action taken in terms of local communities and ending with national and even global solutions (Pawlak, 2006, 2010). With each day, the pandemic impairs people's sense of security and destroys the existing security system. Therefore, all possible tools and measures must be applied to defend ourselves against a similar situation in the future and to prevent the spread of the so-called pandemic of fear.

Conclusions

Access to the use of ISO standards and in many cases the mere existence of pre-implemented systems facilitates the organization of activities for many entities operating globally. What was extremely important was the initiative adopted by the European Commission in March this year on harmonized standards that will allow manufacturers to supply the market with high-performance devices aimed at protecting patients, healthcare professionals and people in general. The standards facilitate, expedite and reduce the costs of the procedure of assessing conformity with European Union requirements. The revised and harmonized standards apply to devices of critical importance, including medical masks, curtains, surgical gowns and suits, autoclaves and sterilization devices (Bokajła, Dziubka, 2003). Stella Kyriakides, EU Commissioner for Health and Food Safety, said: We must not waste a second in our fight against the coronavirus. With the measures we adopt today, we speed up the entry of safe, essential medical equipment and devices such as masks, gowns and suits in the EU market. This equipment is fundamental for our health professionals – the brave and resilient women and men at the front line – to keep saving lives. The presented example clearly shows how European standards are an important pillar in terms of reducing costs, promoting innovation and helping companies access the market. The legal measures used enable the harmonized standards to become part of EU law after they have been agreed on and published in the

Official Journal of the European Union (Weidenfeld, Wessels, 2002). The adoption of such a solution offers a high level of security for users and consumers. As part of this joint effort, the CEN and CENELEC Commission agreed to make a number of harmonized standards applicable for disposable masks and gloves available to companies who want to start manufacturing them. With each day, we receive new, valuable information that raises our level of awareness and teaches us how to act in the new reality. This is why sharing knowledge and offering mutual help at every stage of the pandemic is of key importance. Gaining experience in an organized manner ensures effective defense against various threats, not only during the pandemic. There are many examples of sharing knowledge about the methods of treatment and drugs used among the medical community struggling on the front lines in the fight against the pandemic. The names of such drugs are officially reported in the media; hence, we know that the President of the United States has been receiving remdesivir. Many Chinese doctors have prepared guidebooks describing their experiences in Wuhan and sent them to representatives of medical communities around the world. It was Chinese doctors who at the very beginning of the pandemic reported that the loss of smell and taste is one of the first key symptoms of the disease. Such an attitude is commendable and shows solidarity not only among citizens of a given country, but also among people around the world. With each passing day, we gain more and more experience in the fight against this invisible enemy. On the one hand, we are witnessing a great change and the development of the mechanisms of solidarity and social responsibility, but on the other, the pandemic is attacking and destroying our sense of security. Therefore, every measure possible must be taken to protect humanity from this kind of threat now and in the future. One tool that can help in this regard is the use of ISO standards, especially where they have already been implemented and are already functioning. The international ISO 22301 standard was developed to help organizations build a security system protecting against disruptions to their functioning and reducing the likelihood that various adverse incidents may occur. In addition, it allows a sufficient level of preparedness in order to be able to react quickly and, most importantly, return to normal functioning in the event that such adverse incidents do occur. An important advantage of this standard is the fact that it can be applied in various companies or organizations, regardless of size, location or industry. A structure similar to other ISO standards offers a better understanding and coherence with other management systems such as: ISO 9001 (quality management), ISO 14001 (environmental management) and ISO 27001 (information security management) (Rothery, 1995). Taking into account drastic changes that can occur anytime, organizations with the ISO 9001 or ISO 22301 management systems implemented should strive to improve their defense potential. While country leaders around the world are focusing their full attention on counteracting the threats caused by the pandemic, we cannot forget that we should also be using all possible measures and solutions at our disposal.

References

Bokajła, W. and Dziubka, K. (Eds.) (2003). *Unia Europejska. Leksykon Integracji.* Wrocław: Wydawnictwo Europa.

Fukujama, F. (1997). *Zaufanie. Kapitał społeczny a droga do dobrobytu.* Warszawa-Wrocław: PWN.

Griffin, R.W. (1997). *Podstawy zarządzania organizacjami.* Warszawa: PWN.

Hopej, M. and Kral, Z. (2011). *Współczesne metody zarządzania w teorii i praktyce.* Wrocław: Oficyna Wydawnicza Politechniki Wrocławskiej.

Ishikura, Y. (2007). Act Globally, Think Locally. *Harvard Business Review*, February.

Oleksyn, T. (1997). *Sztuka kierowania.* Warszawa: Wyższa Szkoła Zarządzania i Przedsiębiorczości im. Bogdana Jańskiego w Warszawie.

Pawlak, M. (2006). *Zarządzanie projektami.* Warszawa: PWN.

Pawlak, M. (Ed.) (2010). *Nowe tendencje w zarządzaniu.* Lublin: KUL.

Polski Komitet Normalizacyjny: PN-EN ISO 22301:2020-04.

Polski Komitet Normalizacyjny: PN-EN ISO 9001:2015.

Rothery, B. (1995). *ISO 14000 i ISO 9000.* Warszawa: Agencja Informacji Wydawniczych, IPS.

Weidenfeld, W. and Wessels, W. (2002). *Europa od A do Z, Podręcznik Integracji Europejskiej.* Gliwice: Wydawnictwo Wokół nas.

Wróblewski, R. (2011). Zarządzanie ryzykiem w przedsiębiorstwie. *Zeszyty Naukowe Uniwersytetu Przyrodniczo- Humanistycznego w Siedlcach*, 90.

7 Acceptability and challenges of online higher education in the era of COVID-19

Celina Sołek-Borowska and Adam Ostanek

Introduction

The outbreak of coronavirus disease 2019 (COVID-19) (Shereen et al., 2020) put society into an implausible situation. By the decision of the Ministry of Education in Poland from 11th March 2020, it has been announced that all teaching activities are suspended as from 12th March until 25th March 2020 (https://www.gov.pl/web/edukacja/zawieszenie-zajec-w-szkolach). The decision has been upheld so the summer semester of 2019/2020 has been continued in an online mode.

Following the instructions of the central government, all the state governments in Poland closed all kinds of schools, universities, businesses, traffic, etc. to control the spread of the pandemic. Universities are the key points of social gathering and in this scenario of a pandemic, students and faculty members were forced to live within their houses. Before the outbreak of pandemic, it would be an unimaginable thought to stay at home for a quite long time but it has been the reality now.

Besides the economic and social impacts, there has been a dilemma of accepting the new educational system "e-learning" by students within educational institutions. In particular, university students have to handle several kinds of environmental, electronic and mental struggles due to COVID-19.

In Poland, online teaching is not very popular. Most of the teaching prior to pandemic took place in traditional mode. Most of the teachers were not trained to teach and conduct classes online, either students were not trained at all. Bur considering that younger generation is more skillful in using new technologies, the authors assume that the transformation to online mode was more smooth.

The second motive to undertake this research is such that the research related to COVID-19 has been undertaken to assess the role of digital learning in Pakistani Universities by Shehzadi (2021). Mbambo-Thata (2021) showed how African University responded to COVID-19 in relations to transformation of libraries to digital ones. The research concerning assessment of COVID-19 is scare and needs to be investigated in detail. Therefore, the aforementioned research that undertakes the problem of assessing online

DOI: 10.4324/9781003285717-7

teaching from the perspective of Polish students appears to be appropriate. The main objective of the study is to assess online teaching in Poland, from the perspective of students.

It is worth to highlight that in each country the assessment of online studying will be different. The present study has been conducted under an environment of fear in the society due to pandemic. Immediate shifting from regular to online mode was an unprecedented move.

The chapter is structured as follows: first literature review is presented with the beginning of e-learning in higher education, followed by methodology. Then results are presented. The chapter ends with conclusions and avenues for further research.

Literature review

Beginning of e-learning in higher education

E-learning has been introduced as a fundamental part of the student learning experience in higher education in many developed countries all over the world. It is no longer core business only for those universities with a mission for distance education, its affordances are being systematically integrated into the student learning experience by predominately campus-based universities. Evidence of this widespread uptake can be noticed in reputable research journals which undertake the research of e-learning and on the websites of leading higher education institutions. Examples of these institutions include mainly universities from the UK, the USA and Australia.

To assess online teaching, one must consider challenges, like use of software, hardware, Internet connectivity, etc. Sarrayrih and Ilyas (2013) discussed the various challenges of online examinations. Online assessment may be beneficial for quick, timely and responsive assessment, but issues like assessment of descriptive questions, strategies for different subjects need to be addressed. Ozden et al. (2004) investigated students' perspective of online assessment and found immediate feedback, randomized question order, item analysis of question and immediate scoring as the prominent features of online examination. Baleni (2015) discussed the various benefits of online formative assessment like improvement in students' commitment, faster feedback, etc. Khan and Khan (2019) explored students' perspective of online assessment and found that technological incompetence of students and faculty alongside distrust in technology infrastructure are some points of stress. Stowell and Bennett (2010) found opposite effect of anxiety on students between appearing in classroom examination and online examination.

Developments of e-learning

Keeping the growing demand of online education, a number of online courses have taken place with time. Dave Cormier coined the term "MOOC" for "Massive open online course" in 2008. MOOCs provide an affordable and flexible way to learn new skills, advance your career and deliver quality educational experiences at scale (www.mooc.org). MOOCs have received tremendous response from students worldwide (Rai, 2019). MOOCs provide students an alternative way of getting subject knowledge with certification though online mode. O'Connor (2014) made an analysis of the initial stages of various approaches to MOOCs.

"Open" refers to the fact that the work is out in the open, accessible to everyone. The work presented by the course facilitators as well as the work done by participants is all available for everyone to learn from and reflect on. Rather than completing assignments, students are expected to contribute and engage in the community (MOOC Courses: Massive Open Online Courses [2021 Guide]; mydegreeguide.com). Online courses definitely provided students a huge platform for learning other than classroom yet classroom lectures have their own importance particularly keeping a two-way interaction and clearing doubts of students in mind. O'Neill and Sai (2014) examined the reasons of students for giving priority to face-to-face lectures in comparison to online lectures. Due to the availability of a number of course, modules online, MOOCS have shown a digital revolution in higher education (Kaplan, Haenlein, 2016). A number of universities are offering MOOCS as a supplementary course to the students. Ahmad et al. (2017) in their work provided the statistics of a university where MOOCs are offered as supplementary to higher education. Online education has a great impact on higher education. Students have the facility to choose the best available course for them outside the classroom. Aithal and Aithal (2016) discussed the impact of online education in higher education system. McConnell (2018) presented views of faculty members teaching in Chinese universities about e-learning. Demir (2018) discussed the benefits and challenges of Facebook as an online assessment tool. An effective online learning depends on too many factors like presentation skill, content delivery, use of technology, etc. Crawford-Ferre and Wiest (2012) summarized some effective practices in online instructional methods. Though the online education is growing day by day, yet it has its own challenges (Islam et al., 2015; Swan, 2017).

COVID-19 and higher education

As per UNESCO, on April 1, 2020, education institutions in 185 countries were closed, thus the emergence of COVID-19 affected education globally. Association of Universities (IAU Report, 2020) provided a detailed report of the impact of COVID-19 on higher education across the globe. In this time of crisis, UNESCO (Issue Note 2.4 April 2020a) provided a detailed planning to deal with affect of COVID-19 in education system. UNESCO (Issue Note 4.3 May 2020b) discussed the various strategies adopted by countries to cope up with the current situation. UNESCO has already recommended some parameters for e-learning (Chatelier, Voicu, 2018). In the wake of the COVID-19 pandemic, Polish Ministry of Education has made available the lists of various platforms for digital learning in Poland (Portal Gov.pl, 2020).

Methodology

The online survey was conducted amongst students of Military University of Technology located in Poland. The objective of the questionnaire was to assess the very first experiences of students related to online teaching. The research has been conducted at the Military University of Technology in the month of June and July 2020, which is the ending summer semester for the academic year 2019/2020. The idea was to capture the fresh assessment of online studying for students. This is a quantitative type of research. The target group of students were the students of the Faculty of Security, Logistics and Management. The students have been randomly selected to respond on an online survey using university portals, websites and Microsoft Teams platform. Since the students have been from different masters' and bachelors' programmes of different domains and years, thus the population is heterogeneous.

The sample consisted of 121 students who decided to take part in the research.

The questionnaire consisted of 12 simple questions which aimed to assess the very first experience of online studying, students' feelings towards such form of study, barriers that students notice in such form of study and also the future for online study.

Military University of Technology is a University which is being supervised by the Ministry of National Education and by the Ministry of National Defense. Such situation causes dual regulations imposed by the Ministry of National Defense and Ministry for Higher Education in Poland.

Sample characteristics

The sample was nearly balanced as 51.2% men and 48.8% women took part in the research. Students were diversified in terms of the year of the study which is presented in Table 7.1.

Students were mainly coming from the Security, Logistics and Management Faculty, which comprises 90% of the sample and is presented on Chart 7.1.

The research questions that the authors would like to respond are as follows:

RQ1: How do students assess the experience of online studying?

RQ2: Do students previously participate in online studying?

RQ3: What barriers students experience in online studying

Authors hope that within the following study the questions will be answered.

Table 7.1 Sample characteristics

Year of study and type of studies	*Percentage*
I year bachelor studies	17.4
II year bachelor studies	31.4
III year bachelor studies	18.2
I year master studies	16.5
II year master studies	9.1
I year engineering studies	4.1
II year engineering studies	0.8
III year engineering studies	2.5

Source: Own elaboration (N = 121).

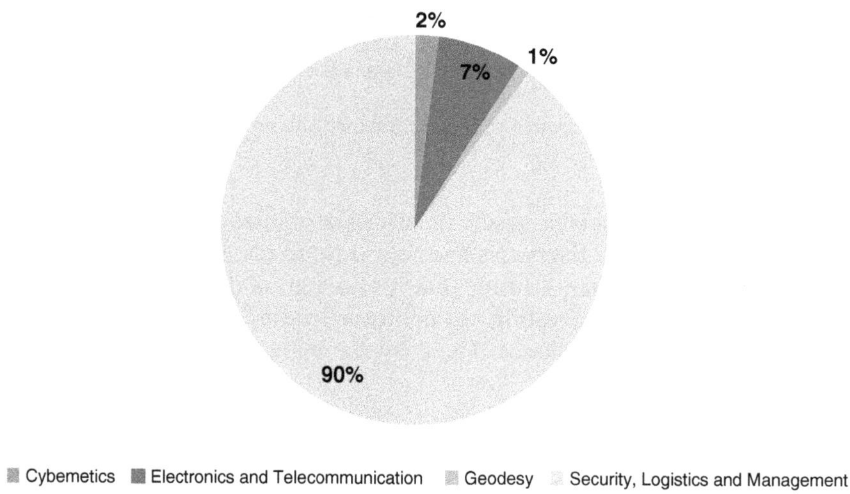

Chart 7.1 The structure of research sample – the criterion of university's faculty.
Source: Own elaboration (N = 121).

Analysis and discussion

Assessment of online studying

Online studying is very different from traditional learning, the shift from conventional pedagogy in higher education to the online mechanism required by teachers to veer their pedagogy. Adapting technology for online teaching within a short span of time was the major challenge for both teachers and students.

Students come to University not only to study but to fulfill their social needs, they make friends, they join different student clubs.

Students were asked whether it was a good decision to introduce online studying. Results are presented in Chart 7.2.

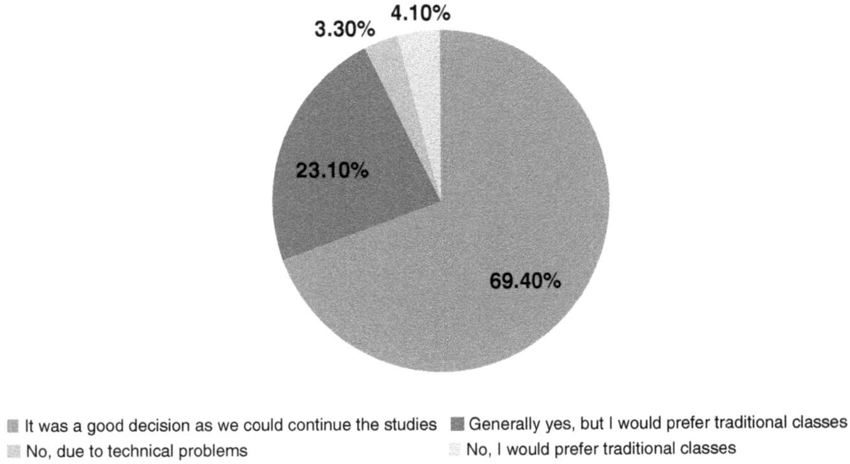

Chart 7.2 Assessment of decision to incorporate online studying.
Source: Own elaboration (N = 121).

Students generally positively assess the decision of introducing online teaching. Although Polish Universities had four days to transfer to online teaching, nearly 70% of students admit that it was a good decision to introduce online studying due to possibility to continue studies. Every fourth student would prefer traditional classes. The answers related to technical problems were expressed by only 3.3%.

When relating to the overall assessment of online studying, students admit that the move to online studying influenced their overall experience of studying, which was expressed by nearly 80% of students, only 22.3% students admit that their studying experience was not affected by the shift to online mode.

When asked about their prior experience to online studying, a great majority of students (84.3%) did not participate in online studying beforehand. Students without prior experience smoothly joined online classes. This is line with the recent conference of Global Business School Network (Home – GBSN) where the head of the Association admitted we did something in three months what we would usually do in three years' time. The results are presented in Chart 7.3.

As the students immediately switched from regular to online mode, it is important to know the comfort level of students with online mode of study. For the majority of students the online classes were taking place for the first time; therefore, it was a natural question to ask about students' overall experience of online studying. Although respondents were asked to assess their overall assessment of online studying, one has to remember that social stress, isolation caused by pandemic affected the overall online studying

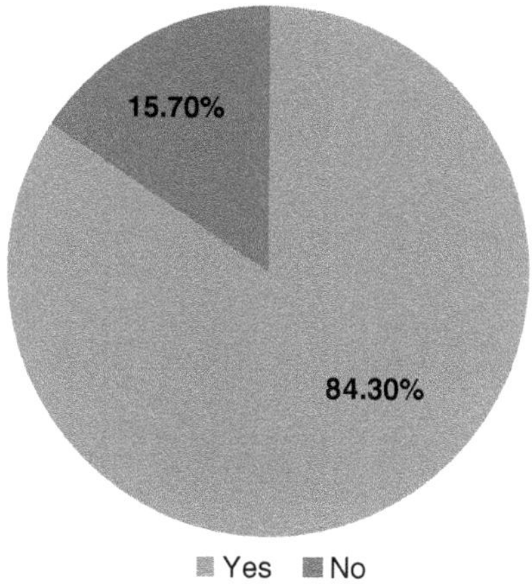

Chart 7.3 Previous experience in online studying.
Source: Own elaboration (N = 121).

assessment. In a regular mode, group discussion and interaction with faculty members help students to clear the concepts, their doubts and understand the subject deeply. Creating the environment of a class is a challenging issue in online education. The results are presented in Chart 7.4.

Nearly 30% of students assess online experience as very good. From the perspective of academic teachers, authors would like to state that students at the beginning liked the idea of chats, camera, hands raising, etc. Everyone believed that online mode will be a temporary one, so the students welcomed a different way of studying. As time was passing on, the students felt more welcoming to come back to a regular mode of study. The decision that the whole semester will take place in the online form was not welcomed positively by the students. Students were asked what platforms are being used. The results are presented in Chart 7.5.

The most popular platform for online teaching is Microsoft Teams expressed by 99.2% of students, this platform was recommended by the University governors, Moodle has gained its popularity amongst 20.7% respondents and Zoom was popular amongst 19% respondents. Online mode has its own requirements, there may be some technical issues that may cause disturbance or delay in a particular task. The intention of the author was to get feedback regarding the problem faced by students in the online studying. Students were asked what are the barriers they experienced in online teaching. Students complained for lack of face-to-face contact, which is exemplified by 47.9% of students, the other answers are presented at Chart 7.6.

Students notice the barriers in online studying but still majority of them would be interested in continuing online studying, such statement was expressed by 56.8% of students but when students were asked about the

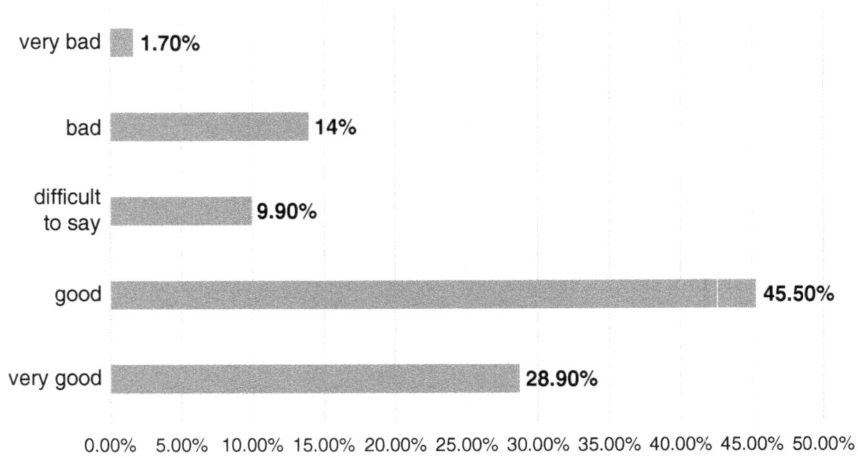

Chart 7.4 Assessment of online studying.
Source: Own elaboration (N = 121).

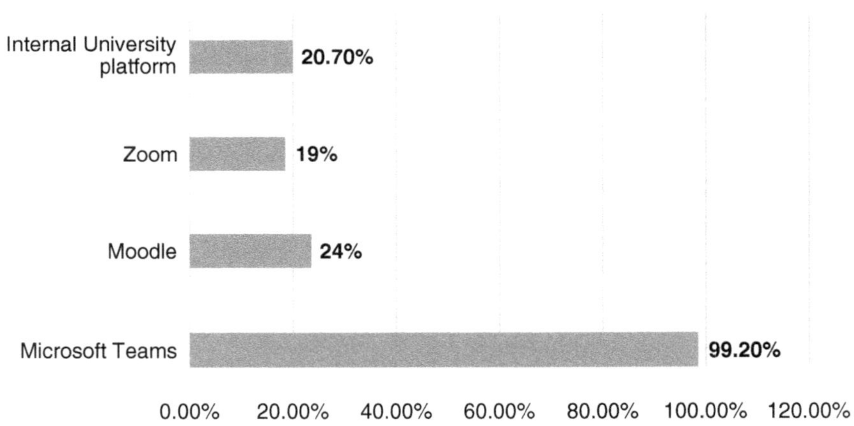

Chart 7.5 Platforms being used in online teaching.
Source: Own elaboration (N = 121).

future of online studying they believe that it should be connected with traditional studying. Around 82.1% of students state that the future of online learning lies in the combination of traditional and online teaching, so the answers are not consistent, and the results are presented in Chart 7.7.

To explain such lack of consistency may be related to the fact that students like some aspect of online studying, but they believe that the future of the University lies in the combination of traditional classes versus online mode. Students are human beings; they have social needs that they want to fulfill. Studying at the University does not involve only academic knowledge, students develop social and networking skills.

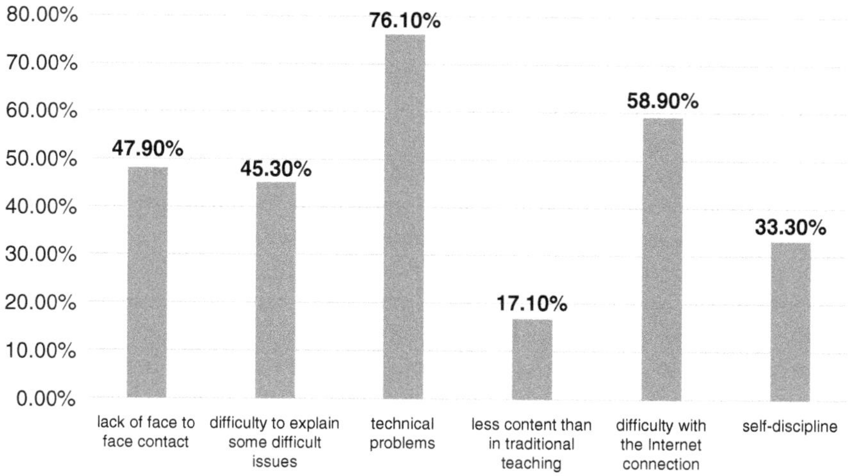

Chart 7.6 Barriers students experience in online studying.
Source: Own elaboration (N = 121).

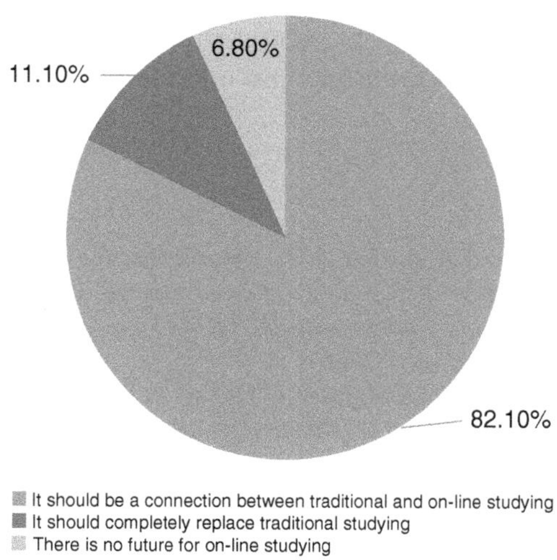

Chart 7.7 The future of online studying.
Source: Own elaboration (N = 121).

Conclusions

The current study provided evidence that students' e-learning is one of the vital elements to provide online education in an emergency situation like COVID-19.

The present study reveals that students moved to online teaching without great problems. The shift was quite smooth. Further, the study shows that the majority of the students have been studying on a regular basis and feeling comfortable with online mode. Internet connectivity and lack of interaction with friends and faculty members are reported as some challenges and concerns for online education. Thus, it can be concluded that the online mode is quite acceptable amongst students with some concerns.

The present study may be helpful in developing standards for online education from regional to global level. The limitation of the study is that the sample represents the view of students from one University. The future research will embrace the comparison analysis of online studying in USA and China in the consideration of the cultural aspect.

The present work was carried out during the initial time of the pandemic in Poland when no well-defined guidelines were there for online education and the focus was to continue the academic process by utilizing all available resources, thus this may be the limitations of the present work in terms of the utilization of resources. At the same time, the following work provides the future scope for studying and analyzing the acceptability with the improved online education as with the passage of time and continuation of online education some standards have been adopted by institutes for improvement in online education.

The current study is most important for universities to start the e-learning system in the current COVID-19 situation, which is leading to the paradigm shift in the education system. Moreover, this study is helpful because the current situation of COVID-19 required a paradigm shift in the education industry.

References

Ahmad, I., Jasola, S. and Anupriya (2017). Supplementing Higher Education with MOOCs: A Case Study. *Proceedings of International Conference on Emerging Trends in Computing and Communication Technologies* (ICETCCT), 1–5. https://ieeexplore.ieee.org/document/8280346.

Aithal, P.S. and Aithal, S. (2016). Impact of Online Education on Higher Education System. *International Journal of Engineering Research and Modern Education*, 1(1), 225–235.

Baleni, Z. (2015). Online Formative Assessment in Higher Education: Its Pros and Cons. *The Electronic Journal of e-Learning*, 13(4), 228–236.

Chatelier, G. and Voicu, I. (2018). E-Learning within the Framework of UNESCO. *Proceedings of the Fourteenth International Conference on eLearning for Knowledge-Based Society.* Thailand.covid19_and_he_survey_report_final_may_2020.pdf.

Crawford-Ferre, H.G. and Wiest, L.R. (2012). Effective Online Instruction in Higher Education. *The Quarterly Review of Distance Education*, 13(1), 11–14.

Demir, M. (2018). Using Online Peer Assessment in an Instructional Technology and Material Design Course through Social Media. *Higher Education*, 75, 399–414.

https://MOOC Courses: Massive Open Online Courses [2021 Guide] (mydegreeguide.com).

https://www.gov.pl.

https://www.gov.pl/web/edukacja/zawieszenie-zajec-w-szkolach.
https://www.mooc.org.
IAU Report (2020). *The Impact of Covid-19 on Higher Education Around the World.* The International Association of Universities. https://www.iau-aiu.net/IMG/pdf/iau.
Islam, N., Beer, M. and Slack, F. (2015). E-Learning Challenges Faced by Academics in Higher Education: A Literature Review. *Journal of Education and Training Studies*, 3(5), 102–112.
Khan, S. and Khan, R.A. (2019). Online Assessments: Exploring Perspectives of University Students. *Education and Information Technologies*, 24, 661–677.
Mbambo-Thata, B. (2021). Responding to COVID-19 in an African University the Case the National University of Lesotho Library. *Digital Library Perspectives*, 37(1), 28–38.
McConnell, D. (2018). E-Learning in Chinese Higher Education: The View from Inside. *Higher Education*, 75, 1031–1045.
O'Connor, K. (2014). MOOCs Institutional Policy and Change Dynamics in Higher Education. *Higher Education*, 68, 623–635.
O'Neill, D.K. and Sai, T.H. (2014). Why Not? Examining College Students' Reasons for Avoiding an Online Course. *Higher Education*, 68, 1–14.
Ozden, M.Y., Ert€urk, I. and Sanli, R. (2004). Students' Perceptions of Online Assessment: A Case Study. *Journal of Distance Education*, 19(2), 77–92.
Rai, L. (2019). Successful Learning through Massive Open Online Courses. *IEEE Potentials*, 38(6), 19–24.
Sarrayrih, M.A. and Ilyas, M. (2013). Challenges of Online Exam, Performances and Problems for Online University Exam. *IJCSI International Journal of Computer Science Issues*, 10(11), 439–443.
Shehzadi, S., Nisar, Q.A., Hussain, M.S., Basheer, M.F., Hameed, W.U. and Chaudhry, N.J. (2021). The Role of Digital Learning Toward Students' Satisfaction and University Brand Image at Educational Institutes of Pakistan: A Post-effect of COVID-19. *Asian Education & Development Studies*, 10(2), 276–294.
Shereen, M.A., Khan, S., Kazmi, A., Bashir, N. and Sddique, R.(2020). COVID-19 Infection: Origin, Transmission, and Characteristics of Human Coronaviruses. *Journal of Advanced Research*, 24, 91–98.
Stowell, J.R. and Bennett, D. (2010). Effects of Online Testing on Student Exam Performance and Test Anxiety. *Journal of Educational Computing Research*, 42, 161–171.
Swan, J.G. (2017). The Challenges of Online Learning. *Journal of Learning Design*, 10(1), 20–30.

8 Mitigating the risk of disruptions caused by the SARS-COV-2 pandemic by schools

Krzysztof Szwarc and Michał Wiśniewski

Introduction

Security is the basic value that should be ensured with combined effort of the citizens, local communities and states. Especially, during the worldwide disasters, when scale and impact is extremely large, states play a significant role in this process.

Based on the law (Journal of Laws, 2019), crisis management consists of preventing crisis situations, preparing to take control over them by way of planned activities, responding in case of emergencies and removing their effects. It means that the ability to prevent and respond to crisis situations like pandemics requires prior preparation, which includes plans, structures, databases and resources necessary to perform crisis management tasks.

Preparation stage includes risk assessment, which is necessary to establish effective risk mitigation strategy. Risk is often expressed in terms of a combination of the consequences of a destructive event and likelihood of occurrence (ISO GUIDE 73, 2009). However, it is very hard to develop systemic approach to describe and to assess both likelihood and consequences in case of a pandemic. Especially, at the state level, where the consequences are complex and difficult to measure.

Therefore, the reaction of security systems in such situations often, especially in the initial phase, seems chaotic and random. According to Solarz and Waliszewski (2020), the response to the pandemic is characterized by a varied rationality characterized by:

- emotions, the level of which changes with reports on the number of cases (especially in the immediate vicinity) and deaths (especially on a mass scale). A specific feature of the analyzed epidemic is the diversified way of feeling the effects of the disease, leading in extreme cases to disregarding the threat or to panic;
- quantitative approach using mathematical models (e.g. SIR/SIRS) to explain and prognosis the phenomenon and to develop an effective strategy of taking control of the spread of the epidemic and technocratic control restrictions of citizens' rights and freedoms;

DOI: 10.4324/9781003285717-8

- economic calculation effort to ensure security in proportion to the short- and long-term economic and social impact of the pandemic;
- demographic variables, where a pandemic may lead to significant changes in the existing aging trends of the population of developed countries, affected by the pandemic.

In such conditions, it is essential to seek mitigation strategies and ensuring the continuity of key services. Regardless of the type of organization, a pandemic can lead to unavailability of (Watters, 2014):

- staff with skills necessary to perform a specific role, where absenteeism may be caused due to (1) fear of getting infection; (2) infection or death due to infection; (3) the need to take care for family members;
- technology used at work, especially information systems that are a specific target of cyber-attacks during a pandemic (INTERPOL Report, 2020);
- buildings in which the work is carried out, e.g. due to the need to disinfect rooms, after identifying an infection;
- personal protection and food products with a long expiry date.

The business continuity impact of a pandemic is particularly apparent in the case of organizations providing services that required the physical presence of the consumer. A particular example of such organizations are schools that have many functions beyond teaching. Continuing the education in remote mode for many parents caused several problems related with the need to provide care for their children, which is difficult to reconcile with the professional duties and has serious economic consequences. This led to research questions:

1 Which school functions have been particularly restricted as a result of the pandemic?
2 How schools dealt with disruptions caused by the pandemic?
3 What can be the consequences of the implemented strategies?

This chapter aims to assess the reaction of selected EU Member States in terms of pandemic. The study will allow assessing the reaction of schools for disruption caused by SARS-COV-2.

Ensuring continuity of education in terms of pandemic

According to Universal Declaration of Human Rights (UDHR), everyone has the right to education and the elementary education shall be free and compulsory (UDHR, 1948). It means that ensuring access to education is one of the basic functions of the modern state.

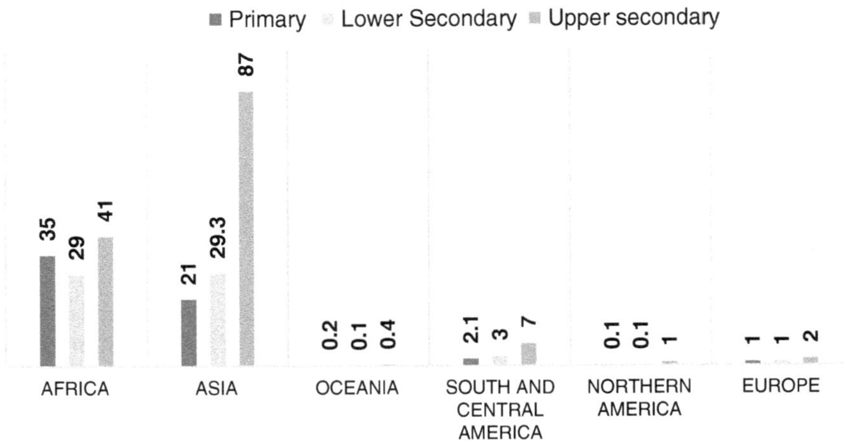

Chart 8.1 Children in the official school age range who are not enrolled in either primary or secondary school (in millions of people).

Source: Own elaboration based on: Global Education Monitoring Report, 2020.

UNESCO (2020) estimates that in 2018 nearly 60 million children did not have access to primary education, especially in the Sub-Saharan Africa and Southern Asia (Chart 8.1). The main causes of exclusion are disability, poverty, migration, belonging to an ethnic, religious or linguistic minority, gender exclusion and distance from school.

A new global challenge has become the need to ensure continuity of education during the pandemic SARS-COV-2. Lack of access to education is a particularly serious problem in the era of the knowledge economy and information and communication technologies called by Alvin Toffler 'The Third Wave' (Toffler, 1994). The possibility of dealing with this problem is quite different in case of highly developed countries and others in case of societies struggling with shortages of basic goods. Therefore, this chapter is limited to the analysis of the strategy of ensuring the continuity of education in selected EU member states.

It is important to define what business continuity really is? Current standard approach states that business continuity should be understood as a capability of an organization to continue the delivery of products and services within acceptable time frames at predefined capacity during disruption (ISO 22301, 2019). It means that (Szwarc, Zaskórski, 2018; Tucker, 2015):

- resilience of an organization is variable and depends on organizational and technical efforts;
- in case of disruption, delays in the delivery of products and services are tolerable, within defined boundaries;
- the quantity and quality of product in such conditions may be limited.

It is necessary to preserve a balance between reliability and cost-effectivity. Consequently, the complexity and cost of risk mitigation strategy should be proportionate to the risk level, what it practically means is that, the reliability of delivery applies only to the key outputs of the system and is limited due to the priority of supply. A key step in business continuity planning is a Business Impact Analysis (BIA). As opposed to the standard approach, the concept of an adaptive approach to business continuity management should be mentioned, the authors of which deny the need for business impact and risk analysis (Lindstedt, Armour, 2017). According to Barnes (2001), Sikdar, (2017), Snedaker and Rima (2014) and Wereda et al. (2016), BIA should provide important information like:

- what products does the organization deliver, who is the customer and what does it expect?
- what processes are implemented in the organization and what is necessary for work?
- what is the organization's appetite for the risk of disrupting business processes?
- what is the relation between the duration of the disturbance and the losses suffered?
- when the organization should resume key processes and when it should restore full operational efficiency?
- who is the provider of the resources necessary for the operation?

The identification of the key product of school is complicated. The concept of school has changed considerably over the years, from closed, isolated fortress, via Marxist perspective as a tool that strengthens disproportions in society to open interacting system, that co-exist in a complex relationship with other socio systems (e.g. Ballantine, Spade, 2008; Chance, 2013; Feinberg, Soltis, 2009; Hoy, Miskel, 2008; Kaplan, Owings, 2017). Brief analysis of mentioned sources and law shows that the basic functions of the school are:

- educational – that enable people to acquire and evaluate knowledge, skills and competences required for a given qualification;
- socialization and upbringing – the process by which a person learns the values, norms and principles in the community;
- support personal development – a process that enables the development of individual talents and abilities;
- care – satisfying material and psychophysical needs necessary for development, as well as ensuring safe conditions for learning;
- cultural – familiarization with the culture of the nation, literature and the most interesting achievements in the arts and music;
- administrative – provides planning, organizing, staffing, leading and controlling.

Services provided by or via schools are considered to be critical for local authorities but does not belong to critical infrastructure at the state level, despite the fact that this is understood as asset, system or part thereof which is essential for the maintenance of vital societal functions, health, safety, security, economic or social well-being of people, and the disruption or destruction of which would have a significant impact (Council Directive 114, 2008). On the other hand, there are examples of good practice regarding the requirements for schools in terms of operational risk management and business continuity planning. An example is the requirements of UK counties which, under the Civil Contingency Act (2004), recommended school management to develop business continuity plans and made suggestions for their creation.

Research method

The subject of evaluation is the way to respond to disruption of the education system caused by pandemic SARS-COV-2 in selected EU Member States. Two hypotheses resulting from the research questions were put up:

- H1. States provided adequate support to the schools at the time of the pandemic.
- H2. Introduction of distance learning in schools significantly affects the risk of a pandemic.

The following criteria were used to assess the impact of government measures to support schools:

- **C1: The beginning of distance learning:**
  - 3 – Before first case;
  - 2 – After first case before first death;
  - 1 – After first death.
- **C2: Established regulations:**
  - Sanitary and hygiene regime;
  - Conditions for changing the teaching mode;
  - Limit the number of students in the classroom;
  - Conditions for conducting the final examination.
- **C3: Forms of support for distance learning:**
  - IT tools supporting distance learning;
  - alternative distance teaching method.

The assessment of the criteria C2 and C3 was conducted on a three-level scale, where:

- 3 – criterion is fulfilled;
- 2– criterion is met partially;
- 1 – criterion is not met.

The evaluation of the introduction of a remote form of education requires taking into account many variables, including:

- V1: impact on the spread of the pandemic;
- V2: impact on the quality of teaching;
- V3: economic, social and political consequences.

In many cases, distance learning is not the only factor causing specific consequences. Remote learning can lead to both positive and negative consequences. Therefore, for the purpose of assessing this phenomenon, an analysis will be focused on the identification of strengths, weaknesses, opportunities and threats (SWOT) related to highlighted variables. The analysis was carried out using surveys of opinions expressed by students, teachers, specialists in the field of psychology, sociology, economics, finance, political and security science.

Findings

A first step was to assess governments' responses to disruptions caused by the pandemic. The study focused on the period between 26th of February, when the first case of infection was confirmed in Austria, and 30th of November, when the second wave of pandemic was found. Table 8.1 shows the results of the research for the summer semester of the 2019/2020 school year.

The research shows that the reactions of the analyzed countries were similar, especially in terms of regulations concerning the organization of the educational process in the new conditions. Some discrepancies related to this criterion concerned the principles of changing the teaching mode and competences to make decisions, which some countries left to the government, and in others to local authorities.

With regard to the first criterion, it should be noted that the decisions of the analyzed countries were made under different conditions (Chart 8.2). Both in Austria and Denmark, the decision to remote teaching was taken after the fatal case was recorded. The analysis of Chart 8.2 shows that in Austria the symptoms of an increase in incidence were properly identified and a decision was made to change the teaching mode immediately before the escalation of the incidence rate. In case of a noticeable increase in the number of cases in Denmark, the decision to change the teaching mode may be considered as belated, which significantly affects the average grade.

The third criterion concerns distance learning support. In case of Poland, in the summer semester in primary and secondary schools, teaching took place primarily with the use of free versions of remote work software, the use of which required a lot of creativity from teachers. It should be noted that after the summer break, Microsoft Office 365 software, including MS

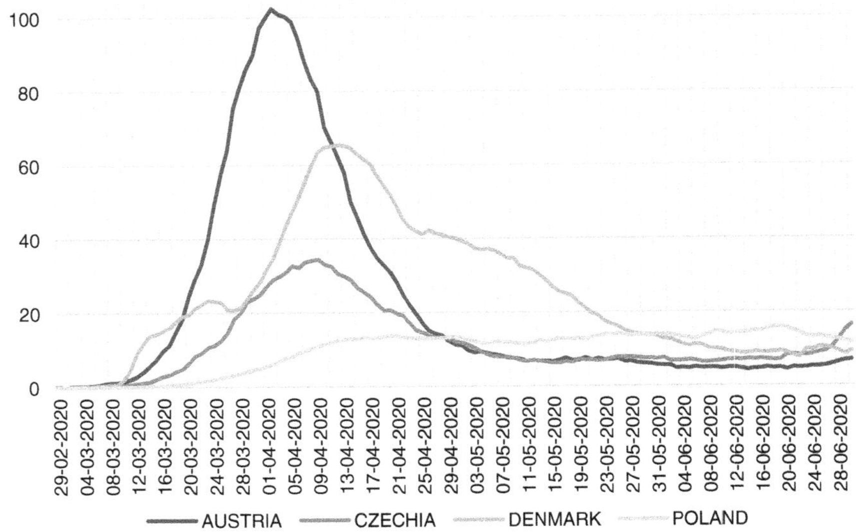

Chart 8.2 Cumulative number for 14 days of COVID-19 cases per 100,000 between 26.02. and 30.06.2020.

Source: Own elaboration based on Eurostat statistics.

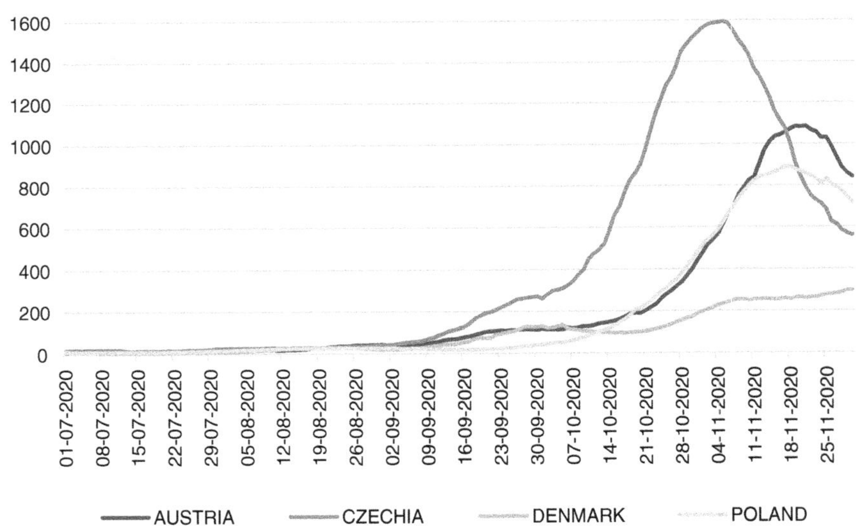

Chart 8.3 Cumulative number for 14 days of COVID-19 cases per 100,000 between 01.07. and 30.11.2020.

Source: Own elaboration based on Eurostat statistics.

Teams, become a standard of teaching. In case of Denmark, there is no information about public television support for distance learning. The study shows that the best support for distance learning among the selected countries was provided in the Czech Republic.

Table 8.1 Aggregate results of the assessment of the governmental support

Issue	*Austria*	*Poland*	*Czech Republic*	*Denmark*
C1: The beginning of distance learning				
First case/fatal case	26.02./13.03. 2020	04.03./13.03. 2020	02.03./23.03. 2020	27.02./16.03. 2020
Start of distance learning	16.03.2020	12.03. 2020	12.03.2020	16.03.2020
Grade:	1	2	2	1
C2: Established regulations				
Sanitary and hygiene regime	Sanitary regime based on hygiene and prevention manual.	Pupils should keep the distance and disinfect their hands and toys. Rooms should be aired and third-party access restricted. The hygiene and organizational recommendations was prepared by Ministry of Education and Main Sanitary Inspectorate.	A special manual specified the rules for: organization of teaching, hygiene, reaction in case of infection, preparation to distance learning. Manual includes essential information and contacts.	Pupils and students have to wash their hands every 1.8–2 hours. Desk should be divided 2 m apart, and children should keep the distance and eat lunch separately.
Reopening conditions	Epidemic risk monitored and presented via four-colour "traffic light system", where red colour leads to switch to distance learning. Most schools gradually reopening on May.	Special care and partial education in kindergartens from 6th of May and primary school (levels 1–3) from 25th of May have been provided. As well as consultations for last year students of primary school.	Schools have been reopened firstly for final-year students (from 11th May) and secondly for primary level of basic schools (from 25th May).	Based on the central government decision, schools have been reopened on April 15. Municipalities may implement the national guidelines flexibly. Schools had to provide the special support for pupils with special educational needs.

(*Continued*)

Issue	*Austria*	*Poland*	*Czech Republic*	*Denmark*
Limit the number of students in the classroom	Classes split in two groups, attending school from Monday to Wednesday or from Thursday to Friday. Special restriction for music education and sport has been established.	Based on ministry recommendations, classes should be reduces and dedicated for children whose parents have problem to combine work and house care.	Maximum 15 students may stay at class, and there must be a statutory declaration confirming the absence of symptoms and other risk factors.	The classes have been limited to smaller groups (10–12) which start lessons at different times. Children and teachers were not required to wear masks.
Conditions for conducting the final examination	Only written test was conducted. The annual grades were included in overall assessment. Oral exams were conducted only on pupil request to compensate for negative assessment. Exams were carried out in compliance with safety and hygiene regulations.	The schedule of final exams in secondary schools was changed. The matriculation examination was conducted between 8 and 29 June. Oral examinations are held only for candidates for studies abroad. The schedule and organization of the matriculation examination were specified by the Central Examination Committee. Examination sheets have been prepared according to the new, changed formula.	The written Czech and foreign language exam has been cancelled. If school education cannot be resumed, the result of the Matura exam should be determined on the basis of the results from three years of study. According to official decree, students in the final year of upper secondary schools cannot be assessed with the grade 'failed' or 'not evaluated' due to the effects of force majeure. Matura and final examinations are taking place starting from 1 June 2020.	The exams were cancelled but education could be prolonged and the final exams being held after schools reopen. Schools may provide a degree and diploma if the student met the required level of knowledge, skills and competences. A diploma issued under such conditions is considered legal and not temporary.
GRADE:	**3**	**3**	**3**	**3**

Forms of support for distance learning:				
IT support	A list of digital tools has been presented on the Ministry of Education's website. Teachers, pupils and parents can use typical or custom communication and storage tools like Office365, G Suite, Moodle, edu. FLOW, LMS.at or SchoolFox. A lot of useful materials have also been provided via digital portals like Eduthek or Edutube.	In most schools, the communication between teachers and children (and their parents) was provided by LIBRUS Platform and open access (or demo versions) tools like ZOOM, Google Hangouts or Skype. At the second period (after summer break) in most regions, some additional support was provided (e.g. Office 365 license for teachers and students). The Ministry of National Educations published a Distance Learning Guide for pupils, parents, teachers and school directors. Some funds were allocated to local government funding to buy some hardware and software.	Actual information about taken measures and graduation schedule is presented on Ministry of Education website. This institution prepared a list of application recommended for distance learning like Bakaláři and popular applications like MS Teams, Skype, Google Hangout or Moodle. The Czech. Based on a result of survey, the Ministry decided to help one thousand selected schools with technical equipment and the use of communication platforms to secure quality online teaching.	The Ministry of Children and Education provided organizational and technical support for schools, like guidelines for distance learning for teachers, that should be based on Microsoft Teams, Skype or Google Hangout Meet, that were available for free. Teachers, children and parents may use typical or dedicated communication ICT tools like Outlook, Aula, Lectio or Ludus.
Alternative methods of teaching	Special support has been provided by the public television ORF.	From the beginning, special support has been provided by the public television (TVP) all channels.	Support has been provided by public television (which launched a dedicated portal and live daily programme) and The Czech Academy of Science.	A solid support was provided by Danish publishers.
GRADE:	**3**	**2**	**3**	**2**
AVERAGE:	**2,33**	**2,33**	**2,67**	**2**

Source: Own elaboration based on: European Centre for the Development of Vocational Training (2020), The World Bank (2020) and governmental websites of highlighted countries.

The H1 hypothesis: 'States provided adequate support to the schools at the time of the pandemic' has been verified by providing that:

- all analyzed countries decided to introduce distance learning based on the analysis of the number of cases;
- in all analyzed countries, the rules of: conducting classes in a remote mode, returning to teaching in a full-time or hybrid mode, examining, maintaining the sanitary and hygienic regime were established;
- in the countries surveyed, different access to equipment and information systems supporting remote work for pupils, students and teachers was observed, as well as differentiated support from the media.

Table 8.2 shows the results of the SWOT analysis. Based on the presented results, it can be concluded that the H2 hypothesis: 'Introduction of distance learning in schools significantly affects the risk of a pandemic' has been verified by providing that:

- distance learning can significantly affect the probability of infection by reducing the number of contacts between people, especially those suffering from the disease in an asymptomatic manner;
- distance learning is conducive to the development of skills related to ICT technologies, but has a negative impact on the acquisition of social competences regarding teamwork, rhetoric and argumentation;
- introducing a remote form of education has various social, economic and political consequences, depending on the age of students, their limitations, infrastructural conditions, quality of access to ICT services, as well as the method of crisis communication.

Conclusions

Ensuring security in conditions of uncertainty is a particular challenge. An attempt to deal with this problem consists in looking for repeatability and expressing uncertain occurrences with the measure of probability and possible consequences. The search for 'measurable uncertainty' [Knight, 1964] is supposed to provide the basis for dealing with threats, formulating certain plans and preparing in case it becomes necessary to use them.

Limited funds for ensuring safety require prioritization and prevention, above all, of such phenomena that occur frequently and have serious, unacceptable consequences. Otherwise, the standard way to mitigate the risk is the therapy, which you also need to be prepared for.

This chapter aimed to assess the reaction of selected EU Member States for SARS-COV-2. Due to the lack of sufficient knowledge about the threat, all governmental decisions in the first phase of the pandemic were made under uncertainty and consisted in the implementation of the therapy mechanism (crisis response and ensuring the continuity of providing socially

Table 8.2 SWOT analysis result

Strengths		*Weaknesses*	
V1	Reduces contact in public transport Limited likelihood of infection at school by students, parents, employees, teachers	V1	Limiting contacts with grandparents Gathering of people in zones recognized as safe Asymptomatic transmission of the disease by young people
V2	Greater accessibility to digital databases, through investment in the purchase of a license by the library The ability to adapt the workplace to individual needs Reducing the cost, time and inconvenience of getting to school Reducing the risk of discrimination on grounds of race, sex, religion and wealth Reducing problems resulting from the failure to adapt school infrastructure to the needs of the education process, including insufficient number of places in classrooms, facilities for people with disabilities Results and progress in education are recorded and archived in digital form Reduction of costs related to education outside the place of residence Reducing the risk of accidents on the way to and from school	V2	Limited access to library resources stored in traditional form The need to abandon the teaching methods that require physical presence Atomization and no sense of belonging to a group Lack of support from people supporting the teaching process Lack or reduced possibility of learning by imitation Difficulties in expressing their views or resolving doubts by shy pupils or students Lack of motivation to choose to learn at the expense of play Limited possibilities of assessing the student's independence Difficulties in delimiting the time spent on study, work and rest Fatigue and lack of discipline Arbitrary leaving the application during classes Interfering with a sense of intimacy, domestic peace disturbance Limitation of mutual support among students

(*Continued*)

Strengths		*Weaknesses*	
V3	Reduction of transport costs and limitations Demonstration of an ability to manage crisis situations Increase in demand for hardware, software and peripherals (cameras, microphones, printers, scanners) Increased demand in the real estate market for houses and large apartments Improving the flexibility of employment Greater integration within the family Increase in the value of companies providing services supporting remote work	V3	Increase of living costs (increase in charges for power, heating, Internet access) Destabilization of the real estate market (limitation of rental services) Limiting relationships with schoolmates or work colleagues Limiting the possibility of acquiring social relations in children with communication disorders and the situational context (e.g. autism, Asperger's syndrome) Increasing the sense of anxiety through isolation Restriction of competition, rivalry The difficulty of combining childcare with work Reduction of excise tax revenues Bankruptcy of companies offering services supporting the education process (e.g. catering, school shop, additional classes) Reduction of employment related to the management of the education process (employees of daycare centres, janitors) Reducing the demand for consumer goods
Opportunities		*Threats*	
V1	The possibility of designating hours when only people from particularly vulnerable groups are served Increasing awareness of the importance of the threat and taking care of your condition and resistance, hygiene	V1	Controlling the presence of children and adolescents in public spaces during school hours Encourages informal, uncontrolled contacts

V2	Strengthens self-learning skills Strengthens the ability to use ICT for teachers and pupils Strengthens the ability to search for and use digital sources of scientific knowledge Reinforces the need for teachers to improve their teaching skills The possibility of greater interest in extracurricular activities Increasing the interest in educating children by parents, including the possibility of observing good practices and identifying bad attitudes of a student or teacher during the education process The possibility of better adjusting the composition of groups due to individual talents Better access to courses from schools and universities abroad.	V2	Weakens cooperation skills Limitation of communication skills Lack of hardware and software necessary for remote learning in poor families or with many children Limited ability to develop psychomotor skills Failure to achieve the desired learning outcome Limited possibilities of ensuring concentration when learning siblings at the same time in one room The risk of disrupting learning due to failure of Internet access Inability to conduct classes remotely Resignation from work of experienced education and science employees due to problems with the remote form of conducting classes Image sharing risk The risk of disclosure of personal data Risk of copyright infringement Risk of disruption of activities by hyperactive children, family members or random events (e.g. renovations) The risk of sharing links to lessons and materials with third parties Risk of posture defects, visual impairment, impairment of physical fitness

(Continued)

Strengths		*Weaknesses*	
V3	Making people aware of showing empathy towards people in need (especially those at risk of a pandemic) Making people aware of showing respect towards people supporting the fight against the pandemic (especially doctors, police, firefighters and rescuers) Development of new technology markets The possibility of increasing trust in state institutions Modernization of ICT Infrastructure in countries Increase in social solidarity Increase in the number of employees with the ability to work on the market of new technologies	V3	Risk of depression, malaise, obesity, lack of motivation Fear of losing civil rights and freedoms Ineffective crisis communication Lack of understanding of the problems and limitations of the remote education system Lack of organizational, normative and financial support for schools and students Reduction in work efficiency due to fatigue, feelings of isolation and routine Ignoring the vulnerability of the elderly to epidemics. Exposing them to infection Limiting involvement in community work and volunteering Increased risk to the confidentiality, integrity and availability of information collected on personal computers Deficit practical skills of candidates to work in certain industries (e.g. medicine, engineering, chemistry, pharmaceuticals)

Source: Own elaboration.

important functions). The renewed increase in the number of infections in the fall (Chart 8.3) proves that the rulers were not able to fully recognize the nature of the phenomenon, nor predict the consequences of their decisions to ease the restrictions.

The inconveniences related to distance education, summarized in Table 8.2, may in part justify the attempts by the government to continue studying in a stationary mode. However, it is difficult to see consistency in action, what is often raised as an accusation against the rulers.

It should be noted that the support provided to the education system, both in the first and subsequent stages of the epidemic, significantly influenced the quality of the education process. Nevertheless, a comprehensive assessment of the mitigation strategies can only be made after the pandemic has ended, as many decisions, including those relating to education, have long-term impact.

The research should be extended to other EU Member States, especially those that: (1) have applied radically different strategies to mitigate the effects of the pandemic; (2) have a much better organized healthcare system; (3) have been particularly severely affected by the pandemic in the first phase.

References

Ballantine, J. and Spade, J. (2008). *Schools and Society: A Sociological Approach to Education*. Los Angeles, CA and other: Pine Forge Press.

Barnes, J. (2001). *A Guide to Business Continuity Planning*. Chichester and other: John Wiley & Sons.

Chance, P. (2013). *Introduction to Educational Leadership & Organizational Behavior*. New York and London: Routledge.

Civil Contingencies Act (2004). legislation.gov.uk/ukpga/2004/36/contents.

Council Directive 2008/114/EC of 8 December 2008 on the Identification and Designation of European Critical Infrastructures and the Assessment of the Need to Improve Their Protection (2008). Official Journal of the European Union L 345/75.

European Centre for the Development of Vocational Training (2020). https://www.cedefop.europa.eu.

Feinberg, W. and Soltis, J. (2009). *School and Society*. New York: Teachers College Press.

Hoy, W.K. and Miskel, C.G. (2008). *Educational Administration: Theory, Research, and Practice* (8th ed.). New York: McGraw-Hill.

INTERPOL Report (2020). *Cybercrime: COVID – 19 Impact*. Lyon: INTERPOL General Secretariat.

ISO 22301 (2019). *Security and Resilience – Business Continuity Management Systems – Requirements*. Geneva.

ISO GUIDE 73 (2009). *Risk Management – Vocabulary*. Geneva.

Journal of Laws of 2019 (2019). *Act of 26 April 2007 on Crisis Management*. Item 1398, 284, 374.

Kaplan, L. and Owings, W. (2017). *Organizational Behavior for School Leadership: Leveraging Your School for Success.* New York and London: Routledge.

Knight, F. (1964). *Risk, Uncertainty and Profit.* New York: Augustus M. Kelley, Bookseller.

Lindstedt, D. and Armour, M. (2017). *Adaptive Business Continuity: A New Approach.* Brookfield: Rothstein Publishing.

Sikdar, P. (2017). *Practitioner's Guide to Business Impact Analysis.* Boca Raton, FL and other: CRS Press.

Snedaker, S. and Rima, C. (2014). *Business Continuity and Disaster Recovery Planning for IT Professionals.* Amsterdam and others: Elsevier.

Solarz, J. and Waliszewski, K. (2020). *Holistic Approach to Systemic Risk Management.* Cracov-Legionowo: edu-Libri.

Szwarc, K. and Zaskórski, P. (2018). The Continuity of Local Governments in Poland during Disasters. *Research and Technology – Step into the Future*, 13(4), 27–34.

The World Bank (2020). https://www.worldbank.org/.

Toffler, A. (1994). *The Third Wave.* New York: Bantam Doubleday Dell Publishing Group.

Tucker, E. (2015). *Business Continuity from Preparedness to Recovery.* Oxford: Elsevier.

UNESCO (2020). *Global Education Monitoring Report. Inclusion and Education: All Means All.*

Universal Declaration of Human Rights (1948). Paris.

Watters, J. (2014). *Disaster Recovery, Crisis Response & Business Continuity. A Management Desk Reference.* New York: Apress.

Wereda, W. et al. (2016). *Intelligent Organization (IO) towards Contemporary Trends in the Process of Management – Selected Aspects.* Warsaw: Military University of Technology.

Index

Note: **Bold** page numbers refer to tables; *Italic* page numbers refer to figures and page numbers followed by "n" denote endnotes.

academic process 106, 108
acceptability: e-learning, developments of 100–101; higher education, e-learning in 100–102; online studying 103–107, *106*
"act globally, think locally" slogan 88
African University 99
Ahmad, I. 101
Aithal, P.S. 101
Aithal, S. 101
Amazon 45
artificial intelligence 67, 70
Association of Universities 101
Asylum and Migration Fund 16
attention 26, 77, 89
Austria 3, 115
autopilot 77
awareness 39, 73; information security 38; manipulation 37; market conditions 73; media disinformation 38–42; situational awareness 33; social awareness 33, 35

Baleni, Z. 100
Barnes, J. 113
Belgium 22, 47
Bennett, D. 100
Berbers-Lee, Tim 68
Black Death 86
brand loyalty 77
budget deficit 26–29
budget surplus 27–28, **28**
business continuity 111, 112; adaptive approach to 113; education sector 111; products and services delivery 112
Business Continuity Management (BCM) 91
Business Impact Analysis (BIA) 113

capital accumulation 21
capital market 4
CEN Commission 97
CENELEC Commission 97
Central Statistical Office 21
children: distance teaching of 74; primary education 112
China 48–49, 93, 108
Civil Contingency Act 114
Client 1.0 (before 1950) 72, 78
Client 2.0 (1950–2000) 72, 78
Client 3.0 (2000–2015) 72, 78
Client 4.0 (2016–2020) 72–73
client–entrepreneur relationship 78–79, **80**
cloud computing 70
collective action 66
collectors 71, **80**
Common Agricultural Policy 16
communication 42, 68, 88
company, monthly revenue 59, *60*
competitive environment 74
computer technology 33
connections 77
consolidation policy 8
consume information 35
consumers: behaviour 60, 78–83; cooperation 65; demand 2; goods and services prices 20, 22; purchasing trends 63; sales channels 61; satisfaction 44, 45, 63; weaknesses 73; *see also* customers
conversation 65
cooperation 66
Cormier, Dave 100

coronavirus pandemic *see* COVID-19 pandemic
Coronavirus Response Investment Initiatives 87
corporate environments 37
cost-effectivity 113
Council Regulation (EC) No 479/2009 23
COVID-19 morbidity 9
COVID-19 pandemic 1; Austria 115; Denmark 115; e-commerce market 43–63; European Union 2–4; French 7–9; Germany 5–7; Italy 9–12; Mongolia 93–96; Poland 19–30; socio-economic effects 2; Vietnam 93–96; *see also individual entries*
COVID-19 vaccination 87
Crawford-Ferre, H.G. 101
creator 71, **80**
credibility 40, 41
crisis management 89, 110
"culture of gift" 71
Customer 5.0 (from 2021) 73
customers *76*; digital age 66–73; and employees 67; evolution of 66–73; purchasing behaviour of 73–78; purchasing decisions **75**; safety and risk 73–78; *see also* consumers
cyberactivism 65
cyberspace environment 37, 40, 41; credibility, information 40; reliability, information 41
Cyprus 22
Czech Republic 116

DAF brand 57, 58, *59*
data analysis 40
decision-making processes 35
Demir, M. 101
Denmark 22, 115, 116
dependent variables 52
developing countries 46
digital age 66–73; client–entrepreneur relationship 78; competitive environment 74; mobile phones 71; reconstruction era 68; *see also* Internet
Digital Commerce 360 45
digital era revolution, disinformation: consume information 35; disinformation and manipulation 36–38; emotional perception 35; fake photos manipulate 35; social awareness 38–42; social consciousness, manipulation 34–36
Digital Europe programme 16
digital risk 78–79, **81**
digital socialism 65
digital transformation 67, 72
digitization process 67
direct corporate income tax 6
Directive on Administrative Cooperation (DAC) 3
distance education 100, 125
distance learning 114–116, 120
domestic demand 20, 21

eBay 45
e-commerce market: in Canada in 2019–2024 **51**; characteristics of 47; in China in 2018–2024 **50**; company, monthly revenue 59, *60*; consumer behaviour 60–63; consumer satisfaction 63; deduction method 44; definition of 45; development dynamics of 45–51; FMCG industry 51–60; in France in 2019–2023 **51**; in Germany in 2019–2023 **51**; in Latin America in 2018–2023 **51**; observation method 44; online sales volume 44; products, categories of *62*; telecommunication tools 45; in USA in 2018–2022 **50**; value of **49**
economic calculation effort 111
economic recession 31
economic slowdown 20, 22
Economic Stabilisation Fund Act 5
educational system 99; continuity of 111; distance learning support 115
e-learning 99; developments of 100–101; in higher education 100–102
electronic articles 61
elementary education 111
emotions 33, 110
employees 67, 90, 92, 93; benefits programme 6; digitization process 67; emotional state of 93; epidemiological safety rules 92; financial support for 8; health and safety of 90; salary of 6
employment 3, 22; contracts, terminations of 10; domestic economy 22; limit mass layoffs 3; subsidies 13; support programmes 9, 10
Enhanced Invest EU 14
epidemiological emergency 92
ESA 2010 methodology 23
EU Member States 22, 23, 24–26, 28, 111, 114, 120, 125; financial support 5;

national budgets 4; support measures 4–5
EU Reconstruction Fund 8
Europe: comprehensive recovery plan 88; national health systems 2; recovery plan for 12–16; strategic challenges 15
European Central Bank 3
European Centre for Disease Prevention and Control (ECDC) 87
European Commission 87; excessive deficit procedure 27; Polish economy 22; public finance sector 19; recovery fund 3; vaccine development 87
European Community Council Regulation (EC) No 479/2009 23
European Council 13, 87
European Investment Bank 3
European Maritime and Fisheries Fund 16
European System of National and Regional Accounts (ESA) 23
European Union (EU) 1; budget in 2021–2024 88; COVID-19 patients 87; COVID-19 vaccination 87; GDP growth rate **21,** 22; global supply chains 2; socio-economic challenge 2–4; sustainable economic development 2; travel restrictions 87; unemployment rate 22
Eurostat data 25
EU State aid rules 4
excessive deficit procedure (EDP) 23
external demand 21

Facebook (FB) 41, 65, 101
Faculty of Security, Logistics and Management 102
fake news 37
false information 33, 38, 39
fast-moving consumer goods (FMCG) sector 44, 47
Federal Employment Agency 6
Federal Labour Office 6
financial balance 26
financial markets 2
financial security 19
Finland 3
First Principles of Disinformation 35
fiscal policy 31
flexibility 3
Fly Research 64n1
France: aid packages 7–8; double-digit recession 8; national health system 7; social cohesion, maintenance of 9
"France Relance" 8
"Frugal Five" 3
Fukushima Daiichi nuclear disaster 90
Fukuyama, Francis 94

general government sector: ESA 2010 methodology 23; expenditure ratio 24; negative balance of 24; revenues and expenditure 23–26, **25**; surplus/deficit 27–29, **28**
Germany 22; direct corporate income tax 6; local authority tax revenue 5; supplementary budget 5
Global Business School Network (GBSN) 104
global Internet space 37
global marketing activities 73
global supply chains 2
goods and services: domestic market of 20; growth rate of 20; market saturation with 73
goods exports 20
Google Trends 47
governmental support, education **117–119**
"green" zones 87
gross domestic product (GDP) 7, 20, 24

healthcare system 5, 7
health insurance 6, 7
higher education: COVID-19 on 101; digital revolution in 101; online education 101
High Representative for Foreign Affairs and Security Policy 34
holistic management concept 91
Hungary 22
hyperarchic structures 65

Ilyas, M. 100
imaginary virtual object 36
"The Independent" 90
individual variables 52
information 35, 73, 74
"information dilemmas" 43
information security 38
information space 37
Instagram 65
insurance 87, 91; *see also* health insurance
Integrated Border Management Fund 16
interlocutors 71, **80**
International Monetary Fund (IMF) 22
international organizations 35

Internet 33, 34, 38, 39, *39,* 41, 42, 45, 46, 47, 68; artificial intelligence 70; cloud computing 70; community 68; connectivity 108; electronic money 70; evolution 68, *69*; online teaching 100; transnational nature of 35; users, categories of 71; Web 1.0 68; Web 2.0 68–69; Web 3.0 69–70; Web 4.0 70
"Internet of Values" 70
interoperability gateway 87
Ireland 22, 25
Ishikura, Yoko 88
ISO 9001 (quality management) 92–93, 97
ISO 14001 (environmental management) 97
ISO 22301:2019 92–93
ISO 27001 (information security management) 97
ISO 31000 risk management standard 91
ISO standards 88–89, 97
Italy 22; employment support 10; wage supplementation schemes 10

Janssen Pharmaceutica NV 87
Japan 89; natural disaster 90; nuclear accident 90; SARS-CoV-2 pandemic 90
Just Transition Mechanism 14

Khan, R.A. 100
Khan, S. 100
Knight, Kevin W. 91
Kolmogorov–Smirnov test 52, **54**
Kremlin 36
Kruskal–Wallis test 52, 54, **54, 57,** 58, **59**

labour market 20, 21, 22, 89
limit mass layoffs 3
liquidity 2–5, 7, 8, 13
loan guarantees 4
local authority tax revenue 5
lockdown 47, 58, 60, 63, 66
loyalty programmes 79

Maastricht fiscal criteria 26, 27, 30
macroeconomic situation 20–22, 28
Mann–Whitney U test 59
Manual on Government Deficit and Debt 23
MAN vehicles 57, *57,* 58
Marian Trench 86
Marxist perspective 113
Mbambo-Thata, B. 99
McConnell, D. 101
McKinsey & Company 74
measurable uncertainty 120
media environment: false information 33; manipulating information 34; psychosocial techniques 34; security gap 33; "trolls" activity 37
Microsoft Office 365 software 115
Microsoft Teams platform 102, 105
Military University of Technology 102
Ministry of Education in Poland 99, 102
mobile phones 71
modern medicine 89
modern technology 34, 76
Mongolia 93–96, 94
MOOC (Massive open online course) 100–101
Moodle 105

National Bank of Poland 20
national economies: protective measures for 4–5
national public finance system 23
Netflix 67
Netherlands 3, 28
New Normal Era 74, 84n1
Next Generation EU 3, 12–13, 16, 88
Nilsen agency 46
non-existent objects 36
non-governmental organizations 35
non-truthfulness 36

observation method 44
O'Connor, K. 101
Omni-commerce 46
O'Neill, D.K. 101
online assessment 100
online education 100, 101, 108
online examinations 100
online sales volumes 44, 45
online shopping 46, 47, *61*; in 2019 and 2020 *48*; consumer satisfaction 45, 63; cyber-attack 77; Poles plan 46; safety of 61; search popularity for *49*
online stores 80, 83
online studying 103–107, *104, 106*; previous experience in 104, *105*
online teaching 99, 100; barriers students experience *107*; Microsoft Teams 105; Moodle 105; Zoom 105
open interacting system 113
organization 88; business continuity management 89, 112; educational process 115; employees of 90–91;

holistic management concept 91; insurance policies 91; quality management 89; risk assessment methodology 91; security 91
Ozden, M.Y. 100

Pakistan 46
Pakistani Universities 99
pandemic control projects 5
Pandemic Emergency Purchase Programme (PEPP) 3
participants 71, **80**
payment services 68
personal data, protection of **82,** 83
personal protective equipment 92
personal trust 40
"persuasive" style 77
physical risks 77
Poland: consumer behaviour 78–83; economic development 20; GDP growth rate 20; goods and services 20; international trade 20; online teaching 99; public finance sector 19–30; social welfare funds 23; tax revenues analysis 23; unemployment rate 22; voivodeship 78
Poles plan 46
Polish government 91
Polish Ministry of Finance 30
Pollack, Todd Dr. 93
portfolio 78
Portugal 22
post-COVID reality: consumer behaviour 60–63
private investment 14
protective measure 92–93
pseudo-anonymous attacks 37
psychological relationship 77
public aid plan 7
public awareness 34
public consciousness 37
public debt management 26, 29, 30
public finance sector: definition of 19, 23; general government sector 23; macroeconomic conditions 20–22; public debt management 26; public finance stability 26–30; security and stability 29; socio-economic development 19; socio-economic strategy 26
public finance stability 26–30
public finance theory 26
public funds 23
public revenues 19, 24; growth rate of 23
public services 30

quality management 89
quantitative approach 110

Radio Free Europe (RFE) 37
Rapid Risk Assessment 87
recapitalisation 5
reconstruction era 68
reliability 41, 113
Rendoo, Davaadorj 94
repeatability 120
research on-line, purchase off-line (ROPO) 73
retail e-commerce sales *50*
retail sales 46
Rima, C. 113
risk assessment methodology 91, 110
risk management 31, 91
risk mitigation strategy 110, 113
Romania 22, 25
Royce, Ed 36
rural development programmes 14

"safe" specializations 89
safety 78
Sai, T.H. 101
sales channels 61, *62,* 63
Sarrayrih, M.A. 100
SARS-CoV-2 virus 1, 86, 111
SCANIA vehicles 57, *58*
schools: basic functions of 113; business continuity 114; concept of 113; government measures 114; risk management 114
Second World War 7
security 91, 93, 110
security gap 33
services 20, 67
sharing 65
Shehzadi, S. 99
shortage 77
showrooming 73
Sikdar, P. 113
Single Market Programme 16
Skinner, C. 70
small and medium-sized French businesses (SMBs) 8
Snedaker, S. 113
social: anxiety 44; awareness 38–42; benefits 6; consciousness, manipulation 34–36; distancing 44; responsibility 94; security funds 24,

27, 29; technological ladder 79, **80**; welfare funds 23
social media 37, 41
socio-economic changes 66
socio-economic development 19
socio-economic strategy 26
Solarz, J. 110
solidarity fund 7
Solvency Support Instrument 14
Southern Asia 112
sovereignty 19
State Treasury debt 29
Stowell, J.R. 100
strengths, weaknesses, opportunities and threats (SWOT) 115, 120, **121–124**
student learning experience 100
Sub-Saharan Africa 112
supplemental oxygen 87
SURE instrument 3
sustainable economic development 2
Sweden 3

tax revenues analysis 23
The Third Wave (Toffler) 112
Thwaites, Guy 93
Toffler, Alvin 112
travel and tourism 2, 93
"trolls" activity 37
trust-building factors 79, **81**
Twitter 41

Ukraine 36
unavailability 111
unemployment 8, 21, 22
UNESCO 101–102, 112
United States 45
Universal Declaration of Human Rights (UDHR) 111
university's faculty 103
US House of Representatives of the Foreign Affairs Committee 36

vaccine 87, 90
value chain layout 88
variability analysis 52
vehicle model 52–54, **54,** *55, 56*
Vietnam 93–96
viewers 71, **80**
VOD (Video on Demand) platforms 67

wage supplementation schemes 10
Waliszewski, K. 110
Walmart 45
Web 1.0 68
Web 2.0 68–69
Web 3.0 69–70
Web 4.0 70
websites 68
well-being 88
Wereda, W. 113
Wiest, L.R. 101
World Health Organization 88, 94
Wuhan 1, 93, 97

YouTube 65

Zoom 105

For Product Safety Concerns and Information please contact our EU
representative GPSR@taylorandfrancis.com
Taylor & Francis Verlag GmbH, Kaufingerstraße 24, 80331 München, Germany

www.ingramcontent.com/pod-product-compliance
Ingram Content Group UK Ltd.
Pitfield, Milton Keynes, MK11 3LW, UK
UKHW020000200926
475702UK00015B/2401
9781032259338